Subhadra Sen Gupta has written over forty books for children because she thinks children are the best readers in the world. She loves telling stories woven around history; plotting complicated mysteries and crazy adventures; dreaming up ghostly tales and scripting comic books. In 2014 she was awarded the Bal Sahitya Puraskar by the Sahitya Akademi for her children's books. If you want to start a conversation with her, send her an email here and she promises to reply: subhadrasg@gmail.com.

Other titles in the series

The Teenage Diary of Nur Jahan, Deepa Agarwal

The Teenage Diary of Jahanara, Subhadra Sen Gupta

The Teenage Diary of Jodh Bai

Subhadra Sen Gupta

talking CUB
An Imprint of Speaking Tiger

TALKING CUB
Published by Speaking Tiger Publishing Pvt. Ltd
4381/4 Ansari Road, Daryaganj, New Delhi–110002, India

First published by Scholastic India (Private) Limited
in 2003
This edition published in Talking Cub by Speaking Tiger
in paperback in 2019

ISBN: 978-93-88874-09-0
eISBN: 978-93-88874-11-3

10 9 8 7 6 5 4 3 2 1

Typeset in Goudy Old Style by Jojy Philip
Printed at Shree Maitrey Printech Pvt. Ltd., Noida

For the Majumdars.
For all the good times, good food and great laughs.
Always with love.

The Teenage Diary of Jodh Bai

The Kingdom of My Father
Raja Bihari Mal
Amber Fort, Rajasthan, 1561
Monsoon to Navaratra

IT RAINED TODAY. Only people like us who live in a dry and dusty desert land know how beautiful rain can be!

All through the summer months of Jyestha and Ashadh the hot winds had blown from the west carrying the sands from the deserts of Jaisalmer, and even when we kept the doors and windows tightly closed, it crept in everywhere, lying like a gritty carpet on the floor. Every afternoon when the harsh rays of the sun turned the upper rooms into hot, airless ovens, we would all retreat into the rooms underground. They were cooler but still not that comfortable. Mother makes her maid Dhanibai fan her as she lies against the cushion, looking tired.

This morning when Dhanibai came to wake up my sister and me, she shook us and whispered, 'Princess, run to the window and look!'

'Why?' I asked sleepily, 'Who's coming?'

'Have the caravans come?' my sister Radhika wanted to know.

Dhani laughed. 'We have visitors from the east!'

'Clouds?'

'Rain!'

The two of us tumbled out of bed and ran to the window to look out. Usually at this time the sky is a flat, washed-out blue, with the sun beginning to glare white. This morning beautiful grey clouds were scudding across like happy messengers. The breeze had turned cool and wet and by mid morning the first, fat raindrops landed in the stone courtyard of the zenana deori where I stay.

All of us poured out into the courtyard–the queens, princesses, maids, all of us stood there happily getting wet as the rain got stronger. I raised my face to the sky and felt the raindrops smack on my closed eyelids; they felt like cool drops of heaven.

Some of the maids had begun to sing and dance, clapping and circling us as they sang of the clouds of Sawan that made the peacock dance. Someone brought out a small drum to keep the beat, the others joined in the singing. Then the queens and princesses joined the circle of dancers, including Radhika and me. I noticed that even Sisodianiji, the elderly queen, was standing in the rain and singing. Watching her, Radhika and I had an attack of the giggles because usually she is such a serious person, she runs the zenana strictly and we are all a bit scared of her. And here she was, the rain running down her face, mixed in the black kohl from her eyes, her hair pasted across her forehead and in her happiness, once in a while, she gave a small skip to the beat of the drums. Rain makes people do mad things, doesn't it?

I am so excited by the rain that I forgot to tell you anything about myself. I should introduce my family to you–after all we are a very special clan, royal and Rajput, and very proud of it too.

My name is Jodh Bai and I am the daughter of Raja Bihari Mal, the King of Amber. We belong to the royal Rajput clan of the Kacchwahas and the Rajputs are the warrior race. They often become kings and noblemen in our region.

There are many other Rajput clans ruling their own kingdoms around us. To the south of Amber is the kingdom of Mewar, with its capital at the famous fortress of Chittor. It is ruled by the Sisodia clan. To the west of Chittor is the kingdom of Marwar, with its capital in Jodhpur, ruled by the Rathore clan. Then, moving even further west, where the land turns into an endless desert, stands the kingdom of Jaisalmer, ruled from their golden fortress in the sand by the clan of the Bhattis. As my mother is a Bhatti princess from Jaisalmer, she is called Bhatiyaniji.

Among them all, the Sisodias of Mewar are the most powerful and respected clan but we are not far behind. My nephew Man Singh says that one day the Kacchwahas of Amber will be the most powerful Rajput clan and also the richest. Well, he hopes to be a king one day and he can do something about it. I am merely a princess and who listens to us? They don't even listen to the queens.

My sister Princess Radhika and I will probably be married into one of these royal families but I don't want to think about it. I just hate the idea of having to leave Amber to go and live in the zenana deori of some strange royal family but what else can I do? I am fourteen already, Radhika is twelve and I know my father is sending out messengers to the royal houses seeking grooms for us. No one will ask me anything, I know. One day I'll be told, 'You are to be married to such and such prince,' and I'll have to smile and go along with that.

Ah well, let's not think about that just yet. I'll enjoy my days of freedom now, and write in my diary.

Two days later

I think I should explain why I am writing in the pages of this notebook that we call a bahi khata. It is making everyone in the zenana deori laugh. All the young girls in the women's quarters of the palace, called the zenana deori, are taught to read and write but no one takes it very seriously. We are princesses and what do we need to do with pen, ink and paper? The most that the older women do is maybe read the holy books sometimes, the Ramayana and the Mahabharata, even for that they can call the Brahmin priest to come and read to them. We are taught the alphabet and a little bit of arithmetic because once we are married we would have to manage our women's households inside our husband's palace and we should be able to check the accounts of the household expenses.

So my sitting down to write made them tease me. Dhanibai said, 'What do you plan to do, Princess Jodh Bai? Write poetry and sing it in the durbar?'

It all began one day when I was feeling bored. It was a very hot day so we couldn't go out to play. Radhika was asleep as she had a fever. So I wandered into the room of Phul Kunwarji, my uncle's wife. Her husband is a prince, a younger brother of my father, the king. The prince is a great fighter and loves to go hunting. He spends most of his time in the nearby fortress of Nahargarh, going off to hunt boar or joining in horse and camel races.

Phul Kunwarji is the youngest of his four wives and I think my uncle does not like her anymore because he never visits her. She is the daughter of a nobleman from the small kingdom of Bikaner and my uncle married her because she is so beautiful. But pretty soon he was off on his hunts again. Phul Kunwarji then was one of the newer women in the zenana and she somehow hadn't made too many friends. She is shy and quiet and spends most of her time in her room in the company of her maids. I like her.

I peered past the carved wooden door into Phul Kunwarji's room. She was alone, I realized with relief. I am a little scared of her maid, a fat, bad-tempered, old woman. She speaks roughly with everyone. The room is furnished like all the other rooms in the zenana—there is a thick mattress laid out on the floor covered with a white sheet. Round bolsters are strewn all over the mattress and there are niches in the wall for the lamps and boxes.

Phul Kunwarji was sitting beside the open window, leaning against a bolster, staring out dreamily. I noticed there was a sheet of paper on her lap and beside her there was the ink tray with the glass bottle of ink and a set of quill pens. She hadn't heard me come in.

'Are you busy, Kunwarji?' I asked from the door.

She turned her head and I thought again, she is so beautiful with soft golden glowing skin, large eyes and curving pink lips. She smiled, 'Oh Jodh Bai! Come in! I'm not busy at all. I'm just whiling away my time.'

I went and sat down beside her. She even smelled nice, of a sweet jasmine perfume. I peered at the sheet of paper in her lap and to my surprise saw it was not a letter at all.

'Oh! I thought you were writing a letter. But

this is a painting! I didn't know you could draw so well!' I looked closely at the half-finished drawing of a woman standing in a garden, with flowers blooming all around her and a deer standing beside a pool of water. Phul Kunwarji was still drawing the lines and hadn't filled in the colours.

'You really draw well.' I smiled at her.

She laughed, 'Well, that is the only thing I am any good at. All the other women in the zenana know so many things–they embroider and weave, cook, sing and dance. All I can do is draw!'

'I can't draw at all. I tried once but my lines are never straight, my faces look like monsters.' Listening to me she laughed and I liked the way her eyes sparkled back at me.

'Want me to teach you?' She picked up a pen and dipped it into the inkpot. 'We could start with simple things, like flowers or trees. Just try, Jodh Bai.' So I obeyed her and tried and tried again. When she drew it was a flower, when I tried the same thing it looked like a rotten cabbage. Her colours were bright and pretty, mine turned to rivers of mud. After a while Phul Kunwarji said gently, 'It's not working, is it?'

I grinned at her. 'I told you, I'm no good but I like doing this.' And I pointed to the pen. 'Dipping my pen into the ink and writing.' Then I showed her the two lines of a poem I had written the night before. I was rather proud of them, the lines even rhymed! I thought them up one morning while standing on the roof of our palace watching the rain clouds come flowing across from the east. Then a peacock had strutted out to the ledge and slowly opened its tail and danced. The lines came to my mind from nowhere,

Dance my pretty peacock, to this cloudy, rainy day,
Like my heart is dancing with the cool raindrops at play.

Phul Kunwarji read the lines and said softly, 'Jodh, this is so beautiful! You must write more.'

'When I was writing this everyone was teasing me. Dhani said I should become a minstrel and travel from village to village singing my poems.'

'They will always tease you.' Phul Kunwarji touched my cheek, 'Don't let that bother you. Women in the zenana have nothing to do, so if anyone is a little different and is happy doing something, it makes them angry.'

'They tease you too?' I asked in surprise, 'But you are a grown-up princess!'

'Of course they tease me.' She laughed. 'But when I paint something they like, they ask for the painting and then hang it in their room.'

'Oh! Of course!' I sat up, 'My mother has this new painting of Lord Krishna in her puja room that she even garlands every day. Did you paint it?'

She nodded. 'Your mother is always very kind to me. So when she said she worships Krishna, I made the painting specially for her.' Once again her eyes sparkled back at me, 'If she garlands it, then she must really like it.'

So that's how I started to write. In the beginning, it was little poems that came to me that I jotted down so that I didn't forget them. Then I wrote about our family. Suddenly I found myself writing about my inner life and the things around me: what I did during the day, the happenings around the zenana, things I heard, my thoughts. It has now become a regular habit with me. Everyone is getting used to it too. Whenever they see me with a pen, paper and my inkpot they just shrug and say, 'Oh! That is silly little Princess Jodh Bai. She likes to waste her time scribbling God-knows-what. No real girl would do that!'

So quite often, not every day of course, I write in my journal. I have even managed to find a small low table that I have placed in a corner of my room, next to a window. The window has a jali screen across it, so the sunlight drifts through it in dancing spots of gold and falls on to the paper. Mother has bought me a lovely inkpot in engraved silver and I went and got a set of pens from the accountant. This old man sits in an antechamber outside the zenana deori and keeps the accounts of all zenana expenses. Most days, he is bent over his desk scribbling long lines of numbers in his bahi khata, the account books bound in red cloth and tied in string.

One morning, I wandered through the courtyards of the deori, with the women's rooms all around. Then I went through the garden to reach the outer rooms. A row of arched doorways led to the room where the accountant sat. The old man has known me since I was a child and I don't veil myself before him.

I strolled up behind him and peered over his shoulder and saw him writing up the hisaab of the shopping of the month—'wheat 5 maan, ghee 20 seer, turmeric 2 seer…' He sensed me standing behind him, and turned slightly and frowned at me, 'Greetings to you, Princess! May I know what brings you here?'

I greeted him back and asked, 'How are you, Munshiji? I hope you are keeping well,' and watching the old man, smiled faintly. I knew I was right to be polite. 'I came to you for some help.' I sat down before his low table.

'My help? What can an old munshi like me do for a princess?'

'Get me some pens.'

'Pens!' he began to laugh. 'Why? You are not

planning to keep the hisaab like me, are you? Count the numbers, add and subtract.'

I shook my head impatiently, 'Of course not! I'm going to write poetry.'

'Ah! Of course! And I have just the right pens for you.' He got up and went to one of the wall shelves and came back with a long, narrow wooden box. Inside, there was a bunch of pens—long, thin pieces of bamboo with one end sharpened to points. He took out four of the thinnest ones with the sharpest points. 'You have ink, inkpot, paper?' He asked briskly. I nodded and told him about the silver inkpot. 'What about paper?'

'I am using the sheets I got from Phul Kunwarji. She uses them for her painting.'

'Oh, those sheets are too thick. They are made especially for paintings, also if you use loose sheets of paper you'll lose them. I have just the thing for a book of poetry.' And he went towards the wall shelves and came back with a bahi khata, just like the one he was using to write his accounts.

I stroked the bright red cloth cover; it was

stitched in place by white threads in a pretty design. Then I opened it and saw the smooth creamy paper inside. All clean and empty and waiting for me to write on them. I sniffed the smell of paper and glue and gave a happy sigh. 'Thank you, Munshiji. This is beautiful.'

'Come to me when you need more.'

'Oh, this will take me ages to fill. There are so many pages.'

'One day you will let me read what you have written? A princess's poetry.' I nodded, returning his smile. 'That would be an honour to read,' he said, bowing to say goodbye.

Tuesday morning

Mother fasts on Tuesdays and only eats after sundown. She does a long puja in the morning that I like to watch. On Tuesdays, Dhanibai wakes me up early so I can have a bath. Radhika usually goes on sleeping but I don't mind. That day, one of the palace singers comes to sing hymns in praise of Lord Krishna in Mother's temple room and the palace priest does the puja.

It was still quite early, and most of the women of the zenana were asleep. Mother and I worked in the puja room, grinding the sandalwood to make a paste, lighting the tall brass oil lamps after filling them with liquid ghee and putting in fresh cotton wicks. The puja room glows gold in their light. We put fresh flower garlands around the dark stone idol of Lord Krishna. He stands there with one foot crossed at the ankle, playing his flute, wearing golden silk garments with fresh sandalwood tilak on his forehead. Krishna is my favourite among all the gods.

The priest came in mumbling his mantras, and dipping a greeting at us, sat down before the altar. Slowly the puja room filled up as quite a few of the women came. There was Dhanibai standing in a corner, ready to help with anything we needed. Also among the women I saw were Phul Kunwarji who flashed me a quick smile, and the calm face of Rukminibai, Man Singh's mother. I wondered what she was doing here, she never came before.

The puja began and in a moment I forgot everything as I sang along with the bhajan singer all the lovely songs in praise of Krishna. Then the priest did the aarti with the many flamed lamps and the room was filled with fragrant incense smoke. Once the puja was over and everyone was leaving, I saw Rukminibai go up to Mother and whisper something into her ear. Mother listened and nodded politely but did not say anything and I noticed that she did not smile. I don't think Mother likes Rukminibai much.

Mother was fasting but called me to have some of the sweets of the prasad. I sat down beside her in her bedroom and she opened out my hair and began to comb and plait it. For some reason Mother just loves to comb Radhika's and my long hair and that is when she talks to us.

'Accha Mother,' I began, still munching a milky barfi.

'Eat the prasad first,' she said firmly.

I swallowed quickly. 'What was Man Singh's mother doing at the puja?'

'She came to pray like everyone else.' Trust Mother to refuse to tell me anything. But I had a feeling it had something to do with my nephew, Man Singh.

All this must sound very confusing to people. Our family is so large and complicated. I realized even Phul Kunwarji, because she does not mix much with the women, was confused. Later that morning, when I was in her room watching her thread a string of pearls, she asked, 'Jodh Bai, who was that woman whispering to your mother in the puja room?'

'Oh, she's Man Singh's mother, Rukminibai.'

'And who is Man Singh?' she frowned.

'My nephew, but he is a year older than me.' I grinned at her puzzled face.

'Nephew?'

'Let me explain,' I said, as we wandered out to the terrace in front of her room. 'You know my father is the King of Amber, he is Raja Bihari Mal. Now he has three queens–the seniormost is the Princess of Mewar, Badana Devi and as she belongs to the Sisodia clan, she is called Sisodianiji. The second, whose name I don't know, is a Rathore princess from Marwar and we call her Rathorainji and my mother, Parvati

Devi, is the youngest and she is a Bhatti from Jaisalmer...'

'...and we all call her Bhatiyaniji. That much I know. But who is Man Singh?'

'I am coming to that... Now we come to the children of the three queens. Sisodianiji is the mother of Prince Bhagwan Das, the crown prince and heir apparent.'

'Oh I see!' Phul Kunwarji brightened up. 'Rukminibai is married to Bhagwan Das and Man Singh is their son and so your nephew.'

'No.' I smiled seeing her all mixed-up. 'Rukminibai's husband was the son of queen number two, Rathorainji.'

'Was?'

'He is dead. Rukminibai is a widow with one son, my nephew Man Singh who is fifteen. You see, my mother...'

'The Princess of Jaisalmer, Bhatiyaniji...'

'...as wife number three, is much younger than the other two queens. My father married her many years later and Radhika and I are her daughters.'

'Still, what was Rukminibai doing in your

mother's puja room? I have never seen her there before.'

I shrugged. 'I don't know. I asked my mother but she wouldn't tell me. It must be something important because the queens usually don't visit each other without first sending a maid to announce their arrival. And Mother never invites anyone to her puja room, except her friends.'

'Like me?' Phul Kunwarji looked delighted. 'She asked me. So I must be her friend.' I smiled back thinking how Mother could make people happy so easily. Among all the women in the zenana she is the only one who is welcome in everyone's room because she never has had fights with anyone–and arguments and fights are pretty common among the women. Even Sisodianiji, who is a very serious person, smiles cheerfully when Mother visits her. As Dhanibai once said, Mother did not give the king a son, only daughters and so, she could have been a forgotten wife like Phul Kunwarji but it is not so. My mother is a very respected queen.

One autumn night

It is early autumn now and the women of the zenana are all busy preparing for the nine-day celebrations of Navaratra. This is a very important festival for the royal family of Amber because we are worshippers of Devi, the Mother Goddess, who brings good fortune and is also a warrior Goddess.

You see, our fortress of Amber is named after the Goddess, Amba Mata. She is a fighter Goddess and we are a fighting Rajput clan. Some people say the fortress was named after her, others think it is named after Lord Shiva, as one of his names is Ambikeshwara. Well, to please both the God and the Goddess, inside the fortress we have temples to both Amba Mata and Ambikeshwara. As Dhanibai says, especially in times when she is upset with the Amber royal family, we always know how to please everyone.

I should tell you a little about Dhanibai. You may think she is just my mother's maid but she is much more important than that. When Mother came to Amber as a young bride from her home in far-off Jaisalmer, she came with a whole entourage of people–maids, cooks, accountant, priest, and these people also brought their families with them.

In Amber, Mother was given her own set of rooms, a puja room and a kitchen. She was given a monthly allowance by my father and with it she pays her people and supervises their work while the accountant does all the hisaab for her. And in fact, Mother leaves most of the work of supervising the other servants to Dhanibai, who, of course, also manages to find time to boss over Radhika and me as much as she can.

Mother and Dhanibai have grown up together. She became Mother's companion when they were children and so they are like old friends. She is married to a soldier and has been given a small house in the village outside the fortress. But she spends her day in our palace, whirling around the rooms like a busy bumblebee buzzing away. And all the while she talks, chattering away with Mother and us. As a matter of fact, if she becomes quiet then Mother begins to worry.

Last evening there was a messenger at the door to tell us that my father was coming to visit us. Father of course, has his own palace outside the zenana deori but he often comes here for his meals. So this night, he would dine with us. Immediately Mother and Dhanibai got busy planning the meal. Radhika and I were asked to wash up and change our clothes and the baithak, the sitting room, was all spruced up.

That night, Father arrives

As Radhika and I were changing our clothes, I asked, 'Radhi, when was the last time Father came to visit us?'

'Long time, many weeks ago. Before the rains.'

'I was beginning to think he may be angry with Mother about something.'

Radhika shook her head. 'He was travelling with the army. There was some trouble at the border with Mewar. They were close to a war.'

'How do you know all this?' I asked surprised.

'Dhanibai was telling Mother all about it. Her husband was there in the battalion travelling with Father. The Mewar army had captured one of our border forts but when they heard that father was coming with a huge army, they quickly left.' She laughed, 'Dhanibai's husband was quite disappointed that they couldn't have a real fight.'

'And what did Dhanibai say?' I grinned in anticipation.

Radhika is a real good mimic and she can copy Dhanibai perfectly. Now, she waved her hands exactly the way Dhanibai does, flapping them before her face and said with dancing eyebrows, 'Oh! These silly men! All they want to do is fight. He even wants to fight the Mughals and then I told him, "You'll get flattened by Akbar Badshah".' And we both collapsed laughing.

It was quite late by the time Father came to our rooms. Mother had wanted Radhika and me to have our dinner on time but we refused. Father likes to eat with us and this was the only time we could be near him.

Father strode in calling, 'Jodhi...Radhi, where are my two pretty princesses?' And we ran up to him to get hugs. He looked at me and said, 'You have grown even taller. How old are you now?'

'Fourteen.'

'Aah! How time flies! Now I'll have to plan your marriage and start looking for a suitable boy.'

'I have a few in my mind,' Mother said.

'I'm sure you do.' He glanced at her. 'And you'll make me listen to you.'

'I'll try.' And they exchanged smiles. They often smile at each other like that, in that odd challenging manner, as if they are competing with each other.

I have seen the other two queens with Father, they are very obedient and modest in his presence. Keeping half their faces hidden behind their veils, and heads bowed, whispering and nodding at whatever Father says. Mother is different. She keeps her face open and looks at Father straight in the eye, she argues with him quite often and listens to him with a critical frown.

I know there are times when Father discusses

matters of state with her, even though she is a woman. They sit together late into the night talking about other kingdoms, the problems of running Amber, the fights within the royal family and Mother offers him her advice. She also makes him laugh often. That is why Radhika and I stay awake when he comes to visit, because it is such fun listening to the two of them when they talk, argue and tease each other.

As always Father, Radhika and I sat down to dinner while Mother and Dhanibai served us. We sat on small square carpets laid on the floor with low wooden tables on which Dhanibai placed the round silver thalis with the food in a circle of katoris. I ate absently, watching Father eat, while Mother sat beside him, serving him the various dishes, the hot bajra rotis, the daal, the fried meats, vegetables.

They make a handsome couple, though Mother is much younger than him. Father's hair and curling moustache are turning grey but the large eyes are sharp as ever and the full lips are firm, like the sharp cheekbones; but he is beginning to get a bit fat and tonight, he looked tired. Beside him, Mother in her pretty red and gold lehenga and chunari, with her eyes darkened by kohl, looked young and full of energy.

As always Father checked out the many dishes and asked, 'What have you cooked? I'd better taste that first.'

Mother grinned, 'And then praise it.' And pointed to the curry of venison, the spicy potato and spinach and the bowl of sweet sewain kheer.

All through the dinner we were talking. Father and Mother of course talk a lot and so does Radhika. I am the quiet one and I only speak in reply to Father's questions. He had a lot to ask about what we are doing.

Mother said, 'Our Jodhi is becoming a poetess.'

'Oh really?' Father looked at me in surprise. 'Let's hear what you have written. I have never had a poet child before!'

I swallowed the roti I was chewing and then recited the two lines I had recited to Phul Kunwarji about the clouds and the dancing peacock.

'Heavens! It even rhymes! This is wonderful,' Father exclaimed.

'Dhanibai says I should become a minstrel and travel across the kingdom singing from village to village,' I muttered moodily and they all laughed.

We were having such a wonderful time. After dinner Father let us stay with him as he sat leaning against a bolster in Mother's bedroom, and as always they began to talk about the state business and politics. Father was telling her about the Mughal King Akbar who ruled from Agra. How he had asked for Father's permission to visit the town of Ajmer which was in our kingdom.

'Why does he want to visit Ajmer?' Mother asked suspiciously.

'It has the shrine of the Muslim saint, the pir, Sheikh Muinuddin Chishti and Akbar is a great devotee of the saint. I have given him permission as a matter of courtesy.'

'Are you sure he won't attack us once he is inside our kingdom?' Mother was still not convinced.

'I don't think so.' Father laughed. 'He will be travelling with a few personal guards and his companions and not his army.'

Then Mother gave Father a paan and said, 'Rukminibai came to visit me again.'

Suddenly Father's happy mood changed and he frowned at Mother, 'Bhatiyaniji, I have told you to stay away from these games. They do not concern you.'

'She came, I did not invite her and Rajaji, I know very well it doesn't concern me.' Mother said briskly. 'After all, I merely have two daughters.'

'Have I ever blamed you for that?' Mother shook her head and stayed silent. Father's voice rose and his face was flushed. 'It was God's will and I don't hold you responsible. Tell my daughter-in-law to stay away. It is not your decision and it is not mine.'

'Not yours?' Mother looked at Father in surprise.

'No, it is for my son Bhagwan Das to decide. He will consult me and my ministers, of course, but the final choice is his. Man Singh's mother knows that very well, why is she coming to you?' Then he and Mother suddenly realized that Radhika and I were still in the room and listening to every word. Mother called Dhanibai and ordered us to bed. Father pulled us closer, giving us big hugs.

'When will you come again?' I whispered, his moustache tickling my face as he kissed me.

'Soon. Very soon, my little poetess.' His voice rumbled in my ears. 'And has your mother got you new dresses for Navaratra? I'll come and see them.'

As Radhika and I followed Dhanibai holding the oil lamp through the dim corridors to our room, Radhika asked, 'What was all that about Man Singh's mother?'

'I don't know, but something is happening. Rukminibai keeps coming to see Mother and sits whispering into her ears. I'll have to ask someone.'

Radhika gestured towards Dhanibai and whispered, 'Ask her?'

I shook my head, 'Phul Kunwarji maybe, or Man Singh if I can catch him the next time he visits the zenana. He'll know what his mother is up to. Dhani won't tell us anything.'

'The women all come to Mother when they want something from Father,' she said thoughtfully. 'After all, there are two older queens, why don't they ask them?'

'They think Father listens to her.'

Dhani turned her head, 'Enough whispering. Now get into bed, you have to get up early tomorrow morning.'

'Oh why?' Radhika wailed. She hates getting up early.

'Because Navaratra starts tomorrow!'

The zenana women love to get excited about things because most of them have so little to do. In villages, women have to cook and clean, work in the fields and walk for hours to fetch water. The zenana women are so spoilt they just wait for festivals like Navaratra to get all dressed up, dance, sing and eat. The nine-day festival of Navaratra ends with Dussehra and then there is Deepavali a fortnight later. These are the most important festivals in Amber and the women prepare for them for weeks–getting new sets of clothes stitched, selecting new jewellery, planning the puja ceremonies. In the kitchens, the cooks are bent over the ovens making hot crispy snacks and a mountain of sweets. The weavers and printers of cloth, the women doing embroidery, the jewellers, the attar maker, all wait at the zenana gate hoping to be called in by the royal women.

The Kingdom of My Father
Raja Bihari Mal
Amber Fort, Rajasthan,
1561

Amber Fort, autumn

ON THE FIRST DAY OF THE nine-day festival of Navaratra, we all went to the temple of Amba Mata to do puja and pray. Early on the first day, the rows of covered palanquins came out of the zenana deori and moved through the palaces to the corner of the fortress where the small temple of the Goddess stands. All the women wearing their best lehengas, the skirts swirling around their ankles, the floating chunari veils over their faces, gold and silver jewellery sparkling, came out of the palanquins in a happy chattering throng and entered the temple. The older women all carried silver thalis, piled high with flowers and fruits that they would offer to the goddess.

Inside, the men of the royal family stood waiting for us. Father stood in the centre, with his son Bhagwan Das, his younger brother, Phul Kunwarji's husband and a couple of his stepbrothers beside them. I know Father is not too fond of these stepbrothers as they keep trying to rebel and take away the throne from him. They live in another fortress and only come to Amber for the Navaratra festival when everyone is very polite to them. As a matter of fact, there are so many stepbrothers, cousins and nephews that I often get quite confused. It is because the men marry so many women, I suppose. The only other face familiar to me was of Man Singh who was lurking behind the men.

Sisodianiji, as the seniormost queen, led the puja with Father, standing beside the priest reciting the mantras. The bells rang, the smoke of incense filled the temple as the family joined in the prayers. This puja goes on for hours, with Father and Sisodianiji sitting down before the sacred fire and pouring ghee into it. It is a very important puja for the family as Amba Mata blesses us with good harvests and victory in war. If the puja fails to please her then the royal family could be in trouble. That is why my father and stepbrothers are so careful that the puja is performed correctly.

After a while I began to feel bored and noticed Radhika also getting restless. Making sure that Mother had not seen us, we crawled away to the back of the crowd and then slipped out of a side door. Away from the noise and smoke, I took a deep breath and looked around. The small temple with the carved pillars and tall, pointed roof was surrounded by shady trees. We sat down on a stone seat under a tree.

'Jodhi,' my sister asked, 'did you notice something?'

'What?'

'During the puja, only the two older queens sat with Father. Why didn't Mother join them?'

I frowned, 'I don't know. She is never asked to do it...I wonder why.'

'Because she has no sons,' said a voice behind us.

We whirled around to see Man Singh peering at us from behind the tree. He had been sitting there all the while listening to us. He wandered over and perched beside me. 'Only the mothers of princes are considered real queens.'

'My mother is a queen,' I protested hotly.

'Only a minor one. The chief queens, the patranis, are from the big royal houses of Mewar and Marwar. Your mother comes from little Jaisalmer and she has no sons. Having a son would have made her a patrani too.'

'If she is so unimportant, why does your mother keep visiting her?' Radhika asked with a sly grin.

'Oh, that's because she wants to get me adopted.'

I looked at his plump face, the quick sharp eyes and said, 'Who'll adopt a fat boy like you?'

'My uncle Bhagwan Das will, if he listens to my mother and grandmother.' We stared at him, very puzzled. 'You two never understand anything, silly girls. My father and Bhagwan Das were stepbrothers, weren't they?' We nodded. 'Now my uncle has no sons. So after him, my father would have been king.'

'But he is dead.'

He nodded. 'That is why my mother wants my uncle to adopt me so that I can become king one day.'

'But why come to my mother?' I asked sarcastically, mimicking Man Singh's superior tone. 'She is just the mother of daughters, isn't she? What can she do?'

'The king listens to her. No one knows why, but my grandfather listens to whatever your mother says. The two senior queens don't like it at all.'

Radhika pinched Man Singh's cheek, 'Poor little boy! Maybe once I am married, I'll adopt you!' Radhika can say such rude things but she says them in such a funny way it makes you laugh. Even Man Singh couldn't help grinning.

Just then, I saw Dhanibai waving frantically at us from the temple door and we went running inside. The puja was nearly over and we had to be there when the priest sprinkled everyone with the holy water saying, 'Om Shanti, peace be with you!' We ran up and stood behind the women and I felt the soft, cool brush of the drops of holy water fall over my face and bent head. When I looked up again, Man Singh had gone off to stand with the men.

Mother, Radhika and I got into our palanquin and sat on the cushions in the curtained wooden box, as the bearers carried us back to the zenana deori. I like riding elephants more; palanquins can be quite uncomfortable, they sway as the men walk and when they are going up or down a hill, they tilt so much that you keep sliding about. Now as we went uphill, we braced ourselves against the sides, clutching the door. Mother was very quiet and didn't even scold us when we began to giggle loudly. She sat holding the curtain open, staring thoughtfully outside. I wondered what had upset her.

That night with Mother

Mother and I were alone in our rooms tonight. Far away I could hear the women singing the Navaratra songs, the beat of the drums and I knew the women were dancing in the deori courtyard. I lay huddled under a thick blanket feeling cold, shivery and feverish. In the evening I had begun to sneeze. Dhanibai touched my forehead and said, 'Get into bed, you have fever,' and fetched a thick cotton blanket.

Mother decided to stay back with me while Dhani took Radhika to the singing. It was taking place in Rathorainji's rooms at the other corner of the zenana deori. 'I'm sorry, Mother,' I said through my blocked nose, 'I have spoiled your Navaratra.'

'No, you haven't.' She came and sat down beside me and began to embroider a pale blue choli for me. 'I did not really feel like going anyway. So your fever gave me an excuse to refuse.'

'But you like to sing!' I protested.

'Only when I am happy,' she said absently.

'Aren't you happy, Mother?' I asked anxiously.

'Sometimes my child, it is very difficult to be a queen. When you marry, you'll know what I'm talking about.'

'What's made you unhappy?' I slid across the bed to rest my head in her lap.

She touched my forehead, 'Your body is still burning. I'd better call the doctor.'

'No Mother, please!' I begged, 'Vaidji will come and feel my pulse and shake his head and then give me those awful bitter syrups. I hate them.'

Mother laughed and stroked my head, 'Theek hai! If you are still running a fever tomorrow morning, then I'll call Vaidji. Now go to sleep.' And as I drifted off to sleep, feeling her fingers running through my hair, I heard her say softly, 'You two are growing up so fast. What will I do when Radhika and you are married?'

I buried my face against her stomach, 'I'm not going to marry.' And I felt her stomach shake as she laughed and then I was asleep.

Next morning

I woke up early and lay there, sleepily staring out of the window. Radhika was still asleep, curled up in a ball beside me. I didn't wake up when she came back last night. She must have tumbled straight into bed as she was still wearing her nice clothes, all crumpled now.

It was just after dawn, the sky going pink, streaking the blue grey of the night. The birds began to call from the trees and I listened to their busy chatter. The pigeons had fluttered on to the ledge outside my window and were busily mumbling deep in their throats, stalking about, waiting for me to come and feed them. Pigeons are my favourite birds, I love listening to them. They are beautiful and a bit stupid and there is a white one with tiny black flecks on her wings that comes and flutters down to peck the grain from my hand. I call them my 'happiness birds' because I always feel happy when I am with them.

Dhanibai was late. The celebrations must have gone on late into the night. I stretched myself under the quilt and lay there dreaming. I felt much better, my nose was clear, though my throat ached a bit. What was surprising was that even Mother was asleep. I remembered our conversation of the night before. Why was she so sad, I wondered. She is usually such a cheerful person, but in the palanquin coming back from the Amba Mata temple, she didn't say a word and once, I thought I saw tears shining in her eyes. She had been fine when we left, dressing up and swishing about looking busy and happy. I remembered I had asked her why she was unhappy and she did not answer my question.

I wandered into Mother's room and it was empty, the bed tidied. I came out into the corridor and looked for her. Even though it was morning it was very quiet, just a few maids wandering around sleepily. I drifted across, peering into the rooms where the royal women were beginning to wake up. The biggest room, with the painted walls and mirrored doors, was the one where Sisodianiji stayed. I've never been inside as she doesn't like meeting people. Phul Kunwarji says the Mewar royal family thinks they are the best among all the Rajputs and that is why she is so snooty. I know Mother is very rarely invited by her and never with Radhika and me. The only people who are welcome are my father and my stepbrother, her only son.

I walked on, still searching for Mother. The next group of rooms was of Rathorainji, Man Singh's grandmother. As I neared the door, I heard voices; one of them was Mother's. I stood still by a latticed window. The older queen was talking. 'He is the king, Bhatiyaniji. He can do anything he wants.'

'I know that. I am just worried about my daughters.' Mother's voice was full of anxiety. 'They are growing up. I want them to be married into good families, Raniji.'

'They will be. He is a good man and he is fond of his daughters. I am certain he will not let you down.'

'I thought that once Bhagwan Das had adopted a son, the matter will be solved. And I thought Man Singh was...'

Rathorainji laughed, 'I have stopped trying to understand the minds of men. The king has only one living son, now he wants more.'

'And I didn't give him any,' Mother said bitterly.

'And my son died,' the queen said quietly. 'It's a blessing that at least I have my grandson.'

I heard my mother sigh. 'So I should prepare myself to welcome her.'

'We welcomed you too once, Sisodianiji and me. This time we three stand together.'

Mother said nothing for a while and then whispered, 'He came to my room recently and he said nothing to me.'

'He is the king, he answers to no one. You'll have to be brave.' Then I heard Mother get up and say her goodbye. I quickly slipped away.

Later in the morning, I was on the terrace feeding the pigeons. The white bird with the black flecks strutted up to peck the grain from my hand but I was not feeling too happy. What had Father done that had made Rathorainji and Mother so angry and hurt? Was it something to do with Man Singh's adoption? Or my marriage plans? Again I thought, I don't want to go away from Amber to go and live in a strange zenana deori full of women I do not even know. I feel so scared every time I think about it. Why couldn't I marry and stay on at Amber, near Mother? Why did Rathorainji say 'be brave'?

'I wish I could fly like you,' I whispered to the

pigeons. 'Then I would fly home from wherever they sent me.'

A week later

Things are happening in the zenana deori and I don't know what it is all about. Man Singh's mother and grandmother seem very busy, with Mother and some of the other women often gathering in Sisodianiji's room. The rest of the time Mother is worried and absent-minded, often not even hearing what I am saying. She sits and broods, eats very little and snaps at Radhika and me even when we haven't done anything wrong. She does not smile at all.

I told Radhika about what I had heard that morning and we have been trying to find out what is happening but no one would tell us anything. None of the other girls in the zenana had a clue. When I asked Dhanibai, she just told me to go and get my hair washed. Phul Kunwarji was just as puzzled and knew nothing. As for Mother, Radhika and I have no courage to go near her. She is usually very easygoing, it is true, but when she loses her temper, she is dangerous. Radhika and I don't like being slapped by her.

One morning I woke up and thought, I'll ask Man Singh. If there is anyone who knows what is happening in the palaces, it is my clever nephew. Also, Rukminibai often talks to her son, who is fifteen and considered quite grown-up.

The problem is that Man Singh no longer stays inside the zenana deori. Once a boy reaches the age of twelve he has to live in the rooms of the men in the outside palaces. I knew Man Singh now occupied the rooms where his father used to stay before he died. The problem was how was I going to find Man Singh? I had to find a way to sneak out of the zenana deori.

It would be most convenient if I could talk to Man Singh when he came to the zenana deori but the problem is that he is never alone when he comes to visit his mother. Usually, he is escorted by Rukminibai's maid from the deori gate and when he decides to visit his grandmother, Rathorainji's maid takes him to her room. If we meet him in the corridors or courtyard, he stops to chat, because we all grew up together, but one of the maids is always standing nearby. Actually, I need the time to have a long chat with him alone.

When we were growing up, there were many children of the queens and princesses to play with, but somehow Man Singh and I always played together. He really hated the fact that even though he was a year older, he was still my nephew. He used to get hopping mad if I called him 'dear nephew' and would yell, 'Call me Man Singh—that is my name, Jodh Bai! I am older than you!'

Now I knew he would explain everything to me. Of course, at the same time he would say I wouldn't quite understand because I was a stupid girl.

So, I had to find my way out of the zenana deori and it had to be early in the morning. I could be sure then that Man Singh was still in his room. He often goes riding and hunting, he also has long lessons of language and mathematics and then goes to learn fighting, using swords, spears and daggers. The boys have to learn much more and it is possible that he will be the king one day. Man Singh himself is convinced he will sit on the royal throne.

For two days, I plotted and planned my escape. Dhanibai was so busy with Mother, worried that Mother is not eating much, that she did not have much time to keep an eye on me. I thought of telling Radhika about my plans but she is too young and is sure to blurt it all out to Mother, and then I would be in deep deep trouble.

From the corner of one of our verandas, you can see the deori gate. So I sat there one morning with my bahi khata, pen and inkpot and doodled on the paper and watched the guards. There were two guards holding spears who checked everyone going in and out. I saw men come up to the gate carrying rolls of paper with messages for the royal women. The maids would collect them and come back with the reply. I saw my stepbrother, Crown Prince Bhagwan Das, get off his horse at the gate and the guards opened it for him.

I leaned out and saw him head for his

mother Sisodianiji's room. There was a lot of movement there, as maids ran in and out carrying trays of sherbet, food and paan. The same thing happened when Father came into the deori, everyone sat up in excitement. I stood there, leaning against the balustrade idly watching a maid, her face covered by a veil, carrying a brass pot of water balanced on her head walk through the garden and head for the kitchen area. Then I had my bright idea! I know now what to do!

Next morning

I got up really early, before Dhanibai arrived, and put on the clothes I had found at the bottom of my clothes' box. The lehenga and choli had faded after a few washes and I had torn one edge of the chunari, when it got caught on a bush while I was playing hide and seek. Mother had told me to give the clothes away to a kitchen maid but I forgot. The kitchen maids are the poorest among the maids. They spend their days chopping vegetables, grinding spices and washing pots and pans. The ladies' maids like Dhanibai are too fancy to wear the faded hand-me-downs.

Just before leaving, I also tucked in a roll of paper at my waist. Then I ran quickly across the main courtyard, slipped through a corridor and got to the second courtyard and ran to the corner of a low gateway that led into the huge kitchen.

I could smell the smoke of the chulhas that were being lit inside to start the cooking of the breakfast.

This kitchen provides the food for the women in the zenana deori. All the people working here are women. The queens have small kitchens attached to their rooms where they occasionally cook a dish or two, like Mother does when Father comes to visit. Otherwise, we all get our food from here. At mealtimes, a row of maids head out of the kitchen bearing huge silver thalis covered with cloth and take the food to the women's rooms.

Reaching the door of the kitchen, I pulled the chunari low over my face, veiling it completely. It hung down to my chin, so nothing was visible.

Then I saw a pile of empty baskets lying in a corner and picked up one and casually walked into the busy room. The huge deori kitchen is an interesting place. Against one wall are a row of chulhas that were now being lit, with maids fanning the burning wood, the billowing smoke filling the kitchen. The smoke helped me, as I was just a veiled shadow floating past and no one paid any attention to me at all.

In one corner, two maids were chopping a mountain of vegetables and chatting. In another corner, two others were bent over huge grinding stones, making turmeric and ginger paste. I stepped over a small hill of potatoes and pumpkins. I didn't want vegetables, I needed fruits. And then I spotted the pile of bananas, papayas and pears. I filled the basket with fruits and, looking very busy, held it high on my head and walked out of the kitchen. My heart was thudding hard but no one asked me where I was taking the basket.

I came to one of the side gates of the deori used by the maids. It had only one guard, an old man busy polishing his spear, who saw the basket on my head and waved me through. I gave a sigh of relief. One problem was over, I was out of the zenana deori. The next one was that I only had a vague idea where Man Singh stayed and would have to find his rooms.

I had been to the palaces of the royal men only a few times in my life. On special occasions, like a visit from other royal families, the women walk through the palaces to sit behind a screen to watch the dance and music programmes in the main palaces. I knew my father's palace and guessed that Man Singh's would be somewhere nearby.

Oh no! I thought in a panic, there were guards at the gate to the main palaces. Now how was I going to sneak in? The guards were sure to ask me questions. I stood hidden behind a pillar and watched the gate for a while and noticed that just past the big gate there was a small opening in the wall that was being used by the servants. I saw men come out carrying baskets of clothes to be washed. Then a row of maids went in with pots of water on their heads. So I quickly ran across and joined the row and went past the door and I was inside the men's palaces, the khas deori.

I looked around. It was similar to the zenana deori but had bigger and more decorated rooms. I stood for a moment and checked my bearings, feeling a bit irritated by the chunari veiling my face. I couldn't see too clearly through the cloth. That is Father's palace, I thought, then the next one must be my stepbrother's. Now does Man Singh stay in those to the other side, or those around the corner?

I wandered up to the door of a large room. There was no one around except a little boy playing by the door. I bent to ask him softly, '*Chhote bhaiya*, does Prince Man Singh live here?'

'Who wants to know?' a firm voice spoke above me and I looked up to see a maid holding a broom staring at me. She was obviously the boy's mother.

'Oh! I'm so sorry!' I stammered, 'Y'see, I have to take these fruits to His Highness's room. These have been sent by his mother...'

The woman frowned and then leaned forward and before I could move back, she had lifted my veil. I felt my heart thud with panic. She let go and said, 'I haven't seen you before. Where is the regular maid of Princess Rukminibai?'

'I...I am new,' I stammered nervously. 'Princess Rukminibai's maid is not well. Please, won't you help me? I'm quite lost.' I tried to sound helpless but I was also feeling very relieved that she had not recognized me. 'Please,' I pleaded, 'I don't want to get into any trouble.'

'*Theek hai!*' she said briskly. Then she pointed to the next set of rooms across the courtyard. 'Go there. And next time Bai, take directions before coming. The guards don't like people wandering about.' I thanked her and quickly walked away before she could come up with any more questions.

When I reached Man Singh's rooms and stepped inside, my way was blocked by his personal servant sitting outside the bedroom door, '*Kya hai?* Where do you think you are going?'

Oh, won't these servants let me go anywhere at all! 'I have brought these fruits for the prince from his mother, Princess Rukminibai.' I said very formally, in very superior tones, the way the ladies' maids speak.

'Fine. Give them to me. I'll give them to the prince.' He held out his hand.

'No bhaiji, I have been told to give them only to the prince and there is also a letter he has to reply to.'

'Let me see it.' I pulled out the roll of paper from the waistband of my lehenga and showed it to him. He opened it frowning and I knew he couldn't read. Finally, he gave up acting superior and let me in.

I walked into Man Singh's bedroom and saw that he was sitting up in bed, looking sleepily towards me, 'Yes?' he said impatiently, sounding very princely.

'Hukoom, these fruits have been sent by the queen mother and...' By then he had sprung out of the bed and was looking curiously at me, 'Who are you?'

'I am just a maid, hukoom...' I began to giggle as he pushed back my veil and his eyes widened in shock, 'Jodh Bai!! What are you doing here?'

'I wanted to meet you alone.'

'I go to the zenana deori every day, Jodh Bai and...'

'I need a private talk.'

'You are mad! If you get caught, do you know what the king would do?'

'Punish me, I know. I have seen the women of the zenana deori get locked up in dark cells without food when they try to run away.' And then it all came tumbling out. 'Mother is in some kind of trouble, Man Singh! No one will tell me anything. I am so worried. I know you will tell me what is what. Man Singh, please!' I pleaded.

Sitting on his rumpled bed, we stared at each other. He looked at me thoughtfully for a long while and then began to laugh. 'God! Jodh Bai! You always were a mad one.' I grinned back, beginning to feel calmer. I knew he would enjoy the idea of me breaking rules, as he is not the obedient sort himself. 'But you can't stay here, the servant will come in and he listens at the door.'

'I told him that you have to reply to a letter your mother sent to you.'

'Wait!' he strolled up to the door and I heard him tell the servant that his mother had summoned him and he had to go immediately to meet her and that his clothes had to be laid out. Then I stood patiently outside his room with my face once again veiled as Man Singh got ready. He came out and said briskly, 'Let's go, Bai.' He strode off with me following obediently behind him. Once we were out of the courtyard, he held my hand and said, 'Let's go! I know the right place where we can be alone...' and we ran.

Man Singh took me on a narrow path that went up the hill behind the palaces and led to a small stone pavilion by the side, looking down into the valley. I panted, climbing and we sat down inside the pavilion. Now we were hidden from view from the palace. He sat down beside me as we looked around at the green hills, the shining waters of the Maota Lake below, the white walls of the palaces and the lovely gardens. The landscape was framed by the deep blue sky above with the dark, wheeling shadows of the eagles who live in high nests on Jaigarh Fort. I could see the old walls of Jaigarh on top of the opposite hill. The fort guards the palaces of Amber.

'This is so beautiful!' I breathed deeply. 'I feel so free now. No walls, gates, guards...'

'I come here when I want to be alone,' he said. 'Sometimes the palace can be so full of people. I found this old pavilion once when I was out riding.' He grinned. 'It is my secret place where I come to hide when I want to avoid my guruji who only wants me to sit and memorise Sanskrit shlokas. You are so lucky you don't have to learn Sanskrit, Jodh Bai!'

A talk in the pavilion

We sat quietly for a while, just enjoying the view. Then I told him about all that was happening in the deori that I didn't understand. He listened silently and then said, 'This will hurt you, Jodh Bai, but you will hear it one day anyway.'

'Hurt me?' I asked, very puzzled.

'Your father, the king, is getting married again.'

I was so surprised I couldn't speak for a while. I stared at him and then said, 'But he is so old! And why? He has three living queens, doesn't he, Man Singh?'

'But he has only one living son.'

'He is marrying again to get a son?'

He nodded. 'Kings marry to get sons. They need many. Children die, grown-up sons get killed in battle. I don't think you know, but he married your mother only after my father died.'

'And she gave him two daughters.'

We sat silently for a while. Now I understood Mother's tears and also her conversation with Rathorainji. Once, the two older queens had welcomed my mother into the zenana deori and now she will have to welcome the new, young bride. I knew my proud mother would not like it at all.

'But what about the prince adopting you? You are a grandson after all.'

'Sisodianiji, the chief queen, has not given her permission yet. She is a proud princess of Mewar and doesn't want her son to adopt me. My mother and grandmother are trying very hard to persuade her.'

'And where is this new queen coming from?'

'She is a princess of Bundi. They say she is only fifteen, my age...'

I thought of Father's greying hair, the lines on his forehead. 'If they marry me off to an old man, I'll take poison,' I said firmly.

'I'll stop them. Don't worry.'

'Hah! Who'll listen to you?'

'They'll listen.' He sounded so confident I could not argue. He does have his way with Father. You trust him to keep his promises. 'One thing I'll make sure of Jodh Bai is that you will marry one of the most powerful kings and he'll be young and handsome too.'

I laughed. 'Powerful kings are all old. How many young kings do you know?'

'There is the Rana of Bikaner and of Jhalawar.'

'Hmmm...'

He clicked his fingers, 'Of course! There is also Akbar, the Mughal King.'

'Don't be mad, he is a Muslim.'

'But he is the most powerful of all and the youngest too. Just twenty and I hear quite handsome too, a big fighter. You could become

Begum Jodh Bai.' By then, he was laughing and ducking from my blows as I hit him really hard.

After a while we began to feel hungry, though I did not want to leave the pavilion. Man Singh frowned. 'Now, how do I get you back inside the deori?'

'I'll go the same way I came, through the back gate by the kitchen,' I said airily. I was feeling very confident of myself.

'I have a better idea.'

Man Singh took me on a long, complicated route that brought us to the back of the zenana deori. We clambered into the deori through a broken window and found ourselves in the oldest part of the women's quarters. Here, all the very old women stayed in tiny rooms. They were the widows of long dead men, unimportant and forgotten women. Here, the walls had not been repaired or painted in years, trees and vines grew everywhere and only a few maids worked around the courtyard.

We peered into dim little rooms where old women sat on rumpled beds, some coughing and smoking hookahs. Others were doing puja and huddling together in patches of sun, gossiping. It was a sad place, so different from our bright and busy courtyard. Man Singh left me at the edge of our courtyard and went back. Pushing back my veil and so turning from maid to princess again, I entered our rooms to find Dhanibai standing anxiously at the door waiting for me.

'Where did you go? I've been looking for you everywhere.'

'I went for a walk,' I said, trying to sound casual. 'Just a morning walk.'

She looked closely at me. 'A walk where? You never go for walks. And why are you wearing that old, faded lehenga and torn chunari?' I really hate it when Dhanibai looks at me like that. She can read my mind, I am sure.

'I went towards the kitchens and then into the old deori.'

'Why? You never go there.' She stared at me frowning. 'Rajkumari Jodh Bai, are you hiding something from me?'

She always calls me by my full name when she is irritated with me.

'I got up early and everyone was asleep and you hadn't come. I was feeling bored, it was all so quiet, so I went wandering about till I got to the kitchens and I watched them cook...' It was sort of the truth anyway. And then luckily Mother called Dhanibai and she hurried inside. I immediately helped myself to the breakfast of puris and potatoes; all the walking had made me ravenously hungry.

A fortnight later

After that chat with Rathorainji, Mother has become much calmer. Now everyone in the palace knows about Father's marriage plans and many of the women secretly laugh about it too. Some of the women have said nasty things to Mother making her cry, but Rathorainji has been very kind to her. Mother goes to her room often and they talk for hours. At times, Rukminibai is also with them.

'How old is Father?' I asked Dhanibai one day.

She gave a bitter smile. 'He is fifty-five and the Bundi princess is fifteen.'

'I'm sure no one asked her if she wanted to marry Father?'

'Of course not! They didn't ask your mother, or Phul Kunwarji. So be prepared, they won't ask you when it is your turn.' I must have looked very scared because she suddenly broke into a very sweet smile and said with concern. 'Don't you have something to write in your bahi khata, little bird? Stop worrying about your mother. She is a Bhatti princess and the Bhattis are brave fighters. She will deal with it.'

Yesterday we were told that the royal procession from Bundi was now close to Amber. The zenana deori had been all spruced up, fresh paint and polish, the garden bushes trimmed, ponds cleaned up. Even the old deori, where the forgotten old women stayed, had been repaired. The kitchen was busy preparing special wedding dishes, the maids had strung garlands and hung them across the doorways.

The Bundi princess, queen number four, would stay in a suite of rooms across the courtyard. I saw the garlands around the pillars, the new colourful carpets on the floor, new furniture and curtains. They said she was bringing a big dowry of jewellery, gold and silver vessels, horses, elephants and camels. Bundi was a small kingdom and they were delighted to make a marriage alliance with the powerful king of Amber. 'And what did it matter if it was someone old enough to be a grandfather?' Dhanibai murmured, as she helped Mother get ready.

Radhika, Phul Kunwarji and I stood on the highest terrace watching the long procession of horsemen, elephants, palanquins and marching soldiers come up the hill path to the fort. Once Mother had come to Amber like this, a new bride, full of hopes and dreams. When the palanquins with the women reached the zenana deori door, we ran down to watch from the courtyard.

Mother, Rathorainji and Sisodianiji, princesses of Jaisalmer, Marwar and Mewar, queens of Amber, stood there to welcome the bride. They all wore their wedding dresses—bright red lehenga-cholis and chunaris covered in gold embroidery. They glittered with jewels—bangles, rings, huge necklaces in gold set with precious stones and thick silver anklets. All three carried silver thalis heaped with flowers, lighted lamps, sindoor and sandalwood. They had lowered their chunaris and veiled their faces, so I couldn't see their expressions. I just noticed how stiffly Mother stood behind the two senior queens. She knew all the women gathered around the courtyard were watching her. The powerful Bhatiyaniji now welcoming a new queen.

'Oh!' said Radhika sounding very disappointed, 'I can't even see her face.'

Phul Kunwarji standing beside her laughed, 'What did you expect? That she would come riding a horse, waving a sword?' And we all laughed.

The tiny figure of the Bundi princess, all swaddled in her wedding clothes, her veil lowered right down to her chest, stood with bent head as one by one, the three queens welcomed her with the aarti. They circled her face with the thalis bearing the lighted lamps and sprinkled flower petals on her bent head. Then she dipped down to touch their feet.

Later, the new bride sat in her chamber as one by one the women went up to her and raised her veil to see her face; sometimes they would comment on her looks and they were not always kind.

One princess said, 'Oh! You have such small eyes, Bundi Rani!'

Another checked her jewellery and said, 'Well, Bhatiyaniji got better bangles from Jaisalmer.'

When Mother went up to her, Radhika and I followed behind. I was dying to see her face. Mother raised her veil and smiled gently at the young face with large, scared, kohled eyes. 'I am the princess of Jaisalmer, they call me Bhatiyani, you can, too. And these are my daughters, Jodh Bai and Radhika. Welcome to Amber, Princess.' The girl gave a shaky smile. Mother touched her cheek. 'Don't be afraid. I live across the courtyard. Come and visit me anytime you feel like. You are as young as Jodh Bai here! My daughters will be your friends.' And at her kind words I saw the eyes of the young princess flood with tears.

As we walked back to our rooms I was right behind Mother and Phul Kunwarji, and I heard Mother say, 'Poor child! Now they'll wait for her to produce a son. They forget the king is old.'

'You feel sorry for her, don't you?' Phul Kunwarji asked curiously.

Mother nodded. She is amazing. I would have thought she would hate a new queen. I know that when Mother came to Amber as a bride, Sisodianiji had been quite cruel to her. Phul Kunwarji spoke again, 'Are you angry with the King?'

Mother's laugh was bitter. 'I am a queen. I obey.'

The Kingdom of My Father
Raja Bihari Mal
Pushkar
Winter, 1561

The month of Kartik

IT HAS BEEN WEEKS SINCE the new queen came to the zenana deori and things have simmered down. She lives very privately, surrounded by her maids and rarely comes out and even when she does, she is veiled. Even though Mother had invited her to our rooms, she has only come once on a formal visit, where she sat surrounded by her entourage of women and said very little. Mother and the older women did all the talking.

Phul Kunwarji says we have to give her time to get used to her new life.

We hear things, of course. We know that Father goes to her rooms often because we see his personal servant, Khem Singh, come to tell the Bundi queen's maid that Rajaji will be visiting. Once he used to bring messages like that to Dhanibai. Father has visited Mother only once and Radhika and I were allowed to go in only to greet him and then we had to leave. He did not have time to eat with us, we were told. Mother was calm but did not smile and spoke very little, quietly listening to Father talk.

A trip is planned

Today Dhanibai came into our room while we were doing our lessons with Sukhwanti Bai. She is an old princess who was once married to some far-off uncle of my father. I can never get these relationships right. Anyway, she is a widow and lives in the old deori. She is very educated and can read and write Sanskrit and even do mathematics. Mother asked her to come and teach Radhika and me because she thinks we two are getting too naughty, spending our days playing in the courtyard. Sukhwanti Bai was trying to teach us grammar and I did not like it at all.

'I would rather write, Baiji. I like dipping my pen into the black ink and then drawing the lines of words.'

She smiled. 'I do, too. It is like painting, isn't it? Only in black and white. It is good that you like to read and write. It will be something you can do after you are married and time hangs heavy. You can fill your days with books and stitching.'

'But I hate stitching!' I said, thinking of Mother. She spends hours stitching our clothes and then doing intricate embroidery on them. Just then Dhanibai came in to say that Mother was calling Radhika and me. We found Mother and Rukminibai sitting together, drinking glasses of sherbet. Mother smiled at us. 'How would you two like to go to Pushkar?'

'Pushkar?' I asked in surprise. It is a pilgrimage to a holy lake. 'Are we going to do puja there?'

‘Or is there a festival?’ Radhika asked.

‘A very special puja.’ Rukminibai was looking delighted. ‘Crown Prince Bhagwan Das has finally decided to adopt Man Singh as his son. Now my mother-in-law, Rathorainji, has decided that we will have the adoption ceremony at the temple of Brahma at Pushkar.’

‘Oh! That is good news!’ Radhika gave a little skip of happiness. ‘Then Man Singh can become king one day!’

‘Maybe…’ Rukminibai said softly. ‘If the Bundi queen has a son, then he’ll also have a right to the throne.’

‘We’ll worry about that when the time comes,’ Mother said briskly. ‘Right now, we have to pack. The girls will need new clothes, too.’

That night

It has become quite cold and the thick cotton quilts have been taken out. Last night I couldn’t sleep, thinking about Man Singh. In the zenana deori his adoption was the main topic of discussion all day. It does not take much to get the women excited anyway, and the question of who will be the next king is very important to them.

So now, after my father Raja Bihari Mal, my stepbrother Crown Prince Bhagwan Das will become king and he will be followed on the throne by my nephew and childhood friend, Man Singh. It pleases me greatly to think of Man Singh as king. He is so clever and he really wants to be a good ruler. Since he was a young boy, he has been preparing himself for it. He has worked hard at his studies and nowadays, even sits in the durbar when Father is working, meeting people, passing judgements and listening to reports from officials. He has also learnt to ride, fight and will one day lead the army.

Man Singh will be a good warrior one day. Father says he is already very good at fighting with the sword. Amber is often at war with neighbouring Rajput kingdoms like Mewar, Marwar and Gujarat, and Father is often away on expeditions to border forts. Man Singh has started going with him and has even done some fighting in the battles. The way he talks about going into battle, I think he likes fighting.

Of course, I know that by the time he becomes king I will be married and living in some faraway kingdom. I often wonder where Father will send me and maybe I won't be able to come to Amber very often. Still, it would be nice to think of my best friend being the king of Amber. It would get me respect in the zenana deori, the way Sisodianiji and Rathorainji get respect because they are related to powerful kings.

Next morning

Man Singh visited us this morning, and if he thought Radhika and I would treat him special, he was most definitely mistaken. Dhanibai came and told us that he was in Mother's room. So we ran in and stood before him, bowing deeply. 'Welcome to our humble abode...' I began sounding exactly like one of the noblemen when they bow and address Father in the durbar. '...Your Royal Highness, Prince of Amber, brave as a lion, handsome as Lord Rama...'

‘Of the great Kacchwaha clan...’ continued Radhika very solemnly as Man Singh broke into a smile, ‘...one day to be king of the great Rajput kingdom of Dhundhar...’

His grin widened, ‘...with his capital at Amber.’ By then, Mother and Dhanibai were laughing loudly and Radhika and I collapsed in giggles.

The durbar

Father decided to announce the adoption in the assembly of noblemen at the royal court. When important durbars are held or announcements are to be made, some of the women are allowed to attend. They sit hidden behind a wooden screen. The three queens, Rukminibai, Radhika and I were given permission to attend.

We all arrived early so that no one saw us, as the royal women maintain very strict purdah. Even Radhika and I had to lower the chunaris over our faces. We walked to the durbar hall and sat down behind the screen. Radhika and I peered out from behind it at the hall with its carpet-covered floor. Father sat on a small, square, silver seat on which was laid a thick silk mattress and round bolsters for him to lean on. On top of his head was a silver umbrella.

As we watched, the hall began to fill with noblemen. All of them were in their best clothes–silk angrakha jackets over their tight churidar trousers with silk patka belts around their waists, a small dagger tucked in. Their proud moustaches flowed across their cheeks–no Rajput ever shaves them off–and on their heads they had tied tall, flaring turbans in bright colours. They all stood respectfully as the usher came to the door and announced loudly that Father was arriving. 'Maharajadhiraj Bihari Mal, King of Dhundhar, Suryavanshi of the descent of the Sun God, Surya...' and he went on for a while praising Father, who entered, followed by Prince Bhagwan Das and Man Singh, looking very royal in a red and gold angrakha and a red turban. On hearing Man Singh's name being announced after the king and crown prince, there was a movement among the nobles as they whispered to each other and then fell silent as Father entered.

As we all listened in silence, Father announced that the Crown Prince had decided to adopt Man Singh and the adoption ceremony would be held at the Brahma temple in Pushkar on the auspicious day of Kartik Purnima. So, the royal family will be travelling there. Then Man Singh was formally presented to the nobles. He looked very serious as he first touched the feet of the King and the Crown Prince and then bowed to the noblemen. The maids came in carrying huge thalis of sweets and everyone began to talk and congratulate Bhagwan Das.

I turned to look at the women sitting behind the screen. Rukminibai was smiling and crying at the same time, wiping her eyes with the edge of her chunari. Rathorainji sat smiling gently with her eyes fixed on her beloved grandson. Beside her sat Sisodianiji, her face still half-veiled. I could only see her lips and they were set firmly in grim disapproval. She had given in to Father's request to allow the adoption but she was not pleased. Mother sat thoughtfully watching the durbar and from her face I couldn't guess what she was thinking.

We are preparing for our trip to Pushkar, packing our clothes and jewellery in large wooden boxes. I heard the Bundi princess is not going with us, but Phul Kunwarji is coming in our entourage. She is very excited because she has not seen Pushkar before and wants to paint the Brahma temple and the holy lakes. So she has packed paper, pen, colours and brushes for the trip. I have taken pen, ink and my bahi khata, which is only half-filled. Maybe I'll write a poem about Pushkar.

Travelling to Pushkar

We started early, just as the sun came up over the eastern horizon. The main gateway to Amber is called Surya Pol, the sun gate, because it faces east and the first rays of the sun touch its red-gold stone and make it gleam. Our Kacchwaha clan is called Suryavanshi, the clan of the sun and so it is considered auspicious to start a journey at sunrise.

The rows of horsemen were followed by our covered palanquins and carts pulled by camels as we moved down the hill to the plains below.

Father, the Crown Prince and Man Singh had their own elephants. Mother, Phul Kunwarji, Radhika and I were travelling in a covered camel cart as they are much more comfortable than the swaying palanquins. We were supposed to keep the curtains closed but Radhika and I had opened them to look out.

It had been months since we had left Amber and we were not going to miss anything. I would have loved to travel on an elephant like Man Singh—he had such a wonderful view sitting high up in his howdah. In the beginning we went through long patches of barren land and craggy hills with small villages but as we neared Pushkar, the fields became green with wheat and golden mustard. Shepherd boys with their flocks of sheep and goats stood and stared at us wide-eyed, and near the villages women stopped their work to run out and watch the royal procession.

We are at Pushkar

We arrived at Pushkar in the evening, and by then I was so tired I just tumbled into bed the moment the tents had been put up. Travelling for miles over bumpy country roads can really make your body ache and it was quite cold too.

Next morning, we all went for a stroll. Pushkar has three lakes and the largest has the temple of Lord Brahma on a hill right beside it. Steps lead down to the lake and we sat there, watching the swans glide past over the crystal-clear water. Phul Kunwarji looked around, her eyes bright behind her veil.

'Do we have to bathe in the lake?' I asked nervously. 'The water will be really cold.'

'The queens have to take a holy dip,' Dhanibai said. 'You can just sprinkle some holy water on your head.'

'Why is the water holy?' Radhika asked.

'Because a petal of Brahma's lotus flower fell into it,' Phul Kunwarji said. 'He is the God of Creation and he fought and killed a demon here, and three petals from the lotus flower that he carries fell from his hand and landed on earth. Three lakes sprang up where the petals fell. That is why this is called Pushkar—"pushp" is flower and "kar" is hand.' She smiled at us, 'Isn't it a lovely story?'

Dhani laughed. 'His fight with Saraswati is not such a happy tale. Getting cursed like that, poor old Brahma.'

Radhika and I turned eagerly towards her. 'Oh please, Dhani, tell us about Brahma and Saraswati.' Dhanibai is a wonderful storyteller and she began, 'Now, you know that Saraswati is the Goddess of Learning?'

'And of music and painting too,' Phul Kunwarji added. 'She is the mother of the holy books, the Vedas.'

'And she is married to Lord Brahma. After he had killed the demon, Brahma decided to hold a big yagna sacrifice here. On the morning of the yagna, everything was ready. The priests, the puja material, the guests had all arrived but Saraswati was still not there. Now, you know that during a yagna, a man and his wife have to sit before the holy fire and chant the mantras together.'

Radhika and I nodded. Sisodianiji always sat next to Father before the fire of the havan when we had a yagna at Amber. 'The auspicious time when the yagna had to start was passing by, but Saraswati was nowhere.'

'What was she doing?' Radhika wondered.

'Dressing up?' I grinned. 'Mother is always late because she can't make up her mind about what to wear.'

Dhani tapped me on the head. 'You are getting too sharp, Jodh Bai. Anyway, to go on with the story, Brahma said that he couldn't wait anymore and asked Vishnu to find him a new wife. Vishnu went and found a cowherd's daughter called Gayatri. She was quickly married to Brahma and the yagna began.'

'Now Saraswati arrives!' announced Phul Kunwarji.

'Yes! Saraswati, all dressed up, arrived and found that a strange woman was sitting next to her husband and she was furious. She has a temper, everybody knows that, and immediately began to curse Brahma. Finally, to calm her down, Vishnu made her sit down on Brahma's right and Gayatri sat on his left. Later, when the temples were built for the two goddesses, they were built at two ends of Pushkar, as far away as possible from each other. We'll visit the temples tomorrow.'

‘What did she say in her curse?’ I wanted to know. Curses can be so interesting and this was a goddess after all!

‘She said that everyone will forget Brahma and no one will worship him. He will only have one temple, here in Pushkar.’

‘That is true?’

‘Yes. There are hundreds of temples to Shiva and Vishnu but there is only one temple to Brahma.’

‘Poor Brahma!’ Phul Kunwarji smiled sympathetically. ‘We must worship him properly tomorrow.’

Kartik Purnima

The full moon of the month of Kartik is believed to be a very auspicious day. So in the morning, we all gathered at the Brahma temple for the formal adoption ceremony of Prince Man Singh.

A big tent had been put up before the temple. After Father, my stepbrother and Man Singh worshipped in the temple. Then they came out and sat before the holy fire of the yagna. To the chant of mantras, Man Singh became the son of Crown Prince Bhagwan Das. I looked at my childhood friend sitting there, the light of the fire falling on his face, blinking a little in the smoke and thought, he'll make a good king. He is intelligent and courageous and he is also kind and caring like my father.

On Kartik Purnima night, there was a special ceremony by the lake. All the women sang hymns to the moon and then we all gathered by the bank of the lake and floated garlands of flowers and small, lighted earthen lamps in tiny leaf plates in the water. It looked so utterly beautiful, I sighed with happiness. There were stars twinkling in the inky black sky and the round, creamy ball of the moon shining in the middle and below, the dark waters of the lake were dotted with tiny, golden points of light as the lamps floated away and the women sang.

Next morning

We are going to stay for some time at Pushkar because Father is going on tour. Whenever the royal family travels, Father and the crown prince use the opportunity to visit the local areas and meet the people. So while we women of the zenana deori stayed happily at Pushkar, they went off with a group of horsemen to visit nearby villages and towns. On these tours, Father talks to the villagers and finds out how his subjects are doing. If they have any problems, they tell him about those problems. It is all very informal, even though these meetings are also called durbars. Father sits in the village squares and the people come up and talk to him. He says, in this way, he makes sure that the officers are working properly and the people are happy. These tours have made Father very popular with the people.

This time, Man Singh is being taken along, as he has to learn the work of a king. He came into our tent to say goodbye and he is very excited about the trip.

'Oh Man Singh! I wish I could go too,' I said dreamily. 'Go riding into the hills and stay in villages. It must be such fun and you won't have to work like Father has to.'

'When I'm king, I'll take you along.' He

grinned, knowing quite well that by then I would be married and far away somewhere, living in the zenana deori of some strange kingdom. I don't expect to be in Amber when Man Singh becomes king.

Winter at Pushkar

Father, Bhagwan Das and Man Singh have been away for weeks now. Our days flow quietly. Phul Kunwarji and I often sit by the lakes, with the warm sun at our backs as she draws and I write in my bahi khata. It feels wonderful being out of the closed-in courtyards of the zenana deori.

This morning, it was cold and misty. The sun was hidden behind the mist that rose like cool smoke from the icy waters of the lake. Phul Kunwarji was wondering how she could paint that on paper and what colours she could use. White or grey or a tint in pale blue? I was watching the swans float in and out of the mist like pale ghosts and thought, they are the vehicles of the Goddess Saraswati, so maybe her spirit does stay at Pushkar.

The royal camp had the women and the

guards and a few noblemen. A large area had been cordoned off for the royal camp and as long as we kept our faces covered, we could move freely inside it. This was why I liked travelling so much. Everyone is more relaxed and the men don't fuss so much about the rules for the women. In Amber, all we hear is 'you can't do this' and 'girls cannot do that'.

Phul Kunwarji and I had reached the edge of the camp where, by the road, there was a small temple of Vishnu and we sat there on the steps, watching the world go by. A little boy went past leading a camel, turning his dark eyes towards us wide in curiosity. I wonder what the villagers think of us, probably as those spoilt, lazy, royal women, who spend their time in idle play. Then a row of village women with shiny brass water pots balanced on their heads came towards us, chattering happily. I watched the way they walked, with proud, easy steps, their lehengas flaring around their legs, teeth gleaming as they laughed and joked with each other,

'You know, sometimes I wish I was born in a village,' I said. 'Don't they look free? I would love to walk around like that, without guards and maids always surrounding me and telling me what to do.'

'You'll also have to work very hard,' Phul Kunwarji laughed. 'Cook and clean and go to fetch water and bring up children, work in the fields...'

'Dhanibai says she'd rather work in a palace than live in a village.'

Just then, we heard the sound of galloping horses and turned to look at the end of the road that led out of Pushkar. First we saw the cloud of dust and then the gleaming spear and tall metal helmets. Then the horsemen came into view.

'These are not our men,' Phul Kunwarji said a little nervously. 'Who are these soldiers?'

'That is not the flag of Amber,' I added.

By then the horsemen were much closer and I could see them more clearly. They wore leather jackets over their cotton tunics and tight trousers. Some of them even had metal breastplates strapped across their chests. They all carried tall spears, some with flags tied to the top, and swords tucked into their belts. The soldiers moved swiftly past with the thudding of the horses' hooves. They took the road to the left that led away from Pushkar. As we watched them vanish in a cloud of dust, I wondered, they did not go into Pushkar. Where were they going?

Many of the guards of the royal camp had come out at the sound of the horsemen and among them, I saw old Bhairon Singh who usually guards the zenana gate. I have known him all my life and don't bother to keep a strict purdah before him. So I raised my veil and asked, 'Bhaironji, who were those horsemen?'

He lowered his lined face thoughtfully at me, his white moustache quivering with disapproval. 'And what are you doing here, so far away from your tent, Choti Rajkumari?' He always calls me Choti Rajkumari, little princess.

'We just went for a walk and I never went outside the camp, Bhaironji. The guards were always nearby.'

'Theek hai.'

'Those soldiers?' I asked again.

'They are the Mughal soldiers of King Akbar.'

'But what are they doing here? Where were

they going? This is the kingdom of Amber.' Phul Kunwarji standing behind me spoke up from behind her veil. 'How can they enter our kingdom?'

'Pranam, Kunwarji,' Bhairon immediately bowed and smiled, recognizing her voice. 'I did think it was you. Those soldiers are going to Ajmer and they have our king's permission to do so.'

'Why? What's there in Ajmer?'

'Ajmer, you know, is very close to Pushkar and it is also a holy city. It has the shrine of the Sufi saint, Khwaja Muinuddin Chishti. Badshah Akbar is a great devotee of the saint. As Ajmer is in our kingdom, he asked Rajaji's permission to visit the shrine to worship there.'

'Badshah Akbar was among the horsemen?' I asked, astonished.

Phul Kunwarji and Bhairon Singh laughed. 'Of course not,' he said. 'Akbar will come a few weeks later and he'll travel in a procession like we do with elephants, horses, carriages and palanquins. These men were the advance guards going to Ajmer to get the place ready for him.'

'Will he go past Pushkar, on this road?' I wondered. 'If we are still here, we could watch the procession.'

The news of the strange horsemen had spread fast and everyone was talking about Akbar at the camp. In the afternoon, many of the royal women, including Mother, were sitting beside the lake basking in the sun. Some were chewing paan, others slicing betel nut, combing each other's hair and tying them in elaborate plaits or doing embroidery. I lay sleepily beside Mother with my eyes closed, listening to their idle talk, their voices drifting around me. They were talking about Akbar.

'I hear he is quite young.'

'He's just twenty. He was barely thirteen when he became king and I heard he's already a great warrior. They say he has never lost a battle so far.'

'His kingdom keeps growing. When he became king, the Mughals only had Dilli and Agra, now his armies have conquered Mandu and Punjab.'

'That is why we are being so nice to him,'

Mother laughed. 'Rajaji immediately gave permission for Akbar to travel to Ajmer.'

'We already have wars with the other Rajput kingdoms, who wants to fight the Mughals too? They have such a powerful army. It would be smart to be friendly with them.' It was Rukminibai's voice.

'But we are Hindus and the Mughals are Muslim,' someone said. 'Can a Rajput and a Mughal really become friends?'

'I think they can,' Mother replied. 'Why not? Akbar may follow another religion but he is human like us. He may make a better friend than some of the Rajputs. What difference does it make if he is a Muslim?'

'Their moustaches are smaller...' I said sleepily, 'Rajputs have bigger ones.' And all the women began to laugh.

A fortnight later

The royal men returned from their tour yesterday. The camp, that had been quiet and sleepy while they were away, woke up to a lot of hustle and bustle because Father was there.

The soldiers polished their helmets and swords and stood straight while guarding the gates. The noblemen marched about looking busy and barking orders. The kitchen was a hive of activity with cooks bent over the fires making the dishes the men liked. In the zenana, the tents were cleaned, the women wore nice clothes and there was less chewing of paan and chatting in the sun.

The biggest problem for Radhika and me was that Dhanibai made us take baths. It was so cold! I didn't even want to get out from under the quilt but she poured ice-cold water over us and scrubbed our faces and oiled our hair. And as we jumped about like grasshoppers and protested loudly, she kept scolding us, 'What are you complaining about? I heated the water.'

'It got cold!' I protested, shivering. 'You heated it a long time ago.'

'Be brave, like a true Rajput princess...'

'We can have a holy bath,' Radhika said through chattering teeth, 'and then we'll catch cold.' Dhanibai just laughed and went on scrubbing us down.

That night

Father came to our tent to have dinner. In the morning his personal servant Khem Singh told Dhanibai that he would be visiting. Hearing that, Mother said with a wry laugh, 'Suddenly he remembers me because the Bundi princess is not here.'

Dhanibai who was sitting in a corner polishing some silver bowls said, 'Rajaji always meets you after his travels.'

Phul Kunwarji who was also in the room smiled bitterly, 'At least he does remember you. My husband has long forgotten he ever married me. If I didn't see him going past my room, I'd forget what he looked like.'

It was quite late when Father finally arrived. Radhika and I were dozing against pillows and Mother was grumbling about the food getting cold. Khem Singh had come once to tell us that Father was sitting with his ministers discussing something important. So Mother made Radhika and me eat and sent us off to bed. I was disappointed at not being able to meet Father but I was so sleepy by then that I couldn't keep my eyes open.

At Amber, with its thick stone walls you cannot hear the conversation in the next room but here, only a thin cloth partition separated us from Mother's room. I don't know what woke me up, but I lay there listening to the deep rumble of Father's voice and then Mother said, 'Have another roti.'

'No, that's enough.' Then I heard Father get up to wash his hands and say, 'Dhanibai, clear up quickly, I need to talk to Bhatiyaniji.'

I must have drifted off to sleep again and woke to hear Mother's raised voice say in surprise, 'Are you sure? He is a Mughal, Rajaji!'

'I am not sure.' Father said, and I could make out he was chewing paan as he spoke. 'That is why I was sitting with my ministers and now I am talking to you. We are surrounded by enemies—Mewar, Marwar, and then my stepbrothers keep trying to capture the throne. I cannot have that Mughal also plotting to attack Amber. He is hungry for new kingdoms to conquer and we are right beside his lands.'

'I'm sure Akbar would like to have the pilgrimage of Ajmer inside his kingdom.'

'Exactly. Also, he wants a free road from Agra to the ports of Gujarat for his trade and that road too goes through Amber. I am surprised he hasn't attacked Amber so far. He worries me, Bhatiyaniji. He is the finest warrior and general among all the kings around us. He has been king since he was thirteen and he and his adviser Bairam Khan defeated everyone they fought with. Bairam Khan may be dead but by now Akbar is an experienced general. He wouldn't think twice about challenging Amber's small army.'

There was a long silence, then Mother said thoughtfully, 'Meeting a Mughal! It is so hard to imagine Amber becoming an ally of Akbar. He is a Muslim too, the other Rajput kings won't like it at all.'

Father laughed, 'Bhatiyaniji, our greatest enemies are all Rajputs!'

Finally, I was beginning to understand what they were talking about. Father was planning to meet Akbar and offer him his friendship. In this way, as allies, he hoped Akbar would not attack Amber, and also that Akbar would help Father against his enemies.

Mother spoke again, 'So what do you plan to do?'

'Akbar is leaving Agra in a few days to travel to Ajmer on his pilgrimage. On the way, he will be staying at Deosa. I will send a messenger tomorrow requesting that I be allowed to meet him there.'

'What did the Crown Prince and the ministers say?'

'Many of the older ones were against it as they all fought Akbar's grandfather, Babur, at the Battle of Khanua.'

'And they lost,' Mother said shortly. 'Even when all the Rajputs united under Rana Sangram Singh, they still lost to Babur.'

'That is what I told them. What can Amber do alone and we will be the first to be attacked. I have no hope that the other kings will come to help me.'

'That has always been our problem,' Mother's voice sounded sad. 'We are brave and great fighters, but we spend our time fighting each other. We have never learnt to unite. That is why the invaders always win.'

I could hear Father move around the room. He was pacing restlessly and I could at times see his shadow fall on the cloth partition. 'So you agree it is the right thing for me to do?'

'Rajaji, you need to meet Badshah Akbar. This is the right time, when he is feeling grateful to you for allowing him to visit Ajmer. You have to talk to him, find out what kind of a person he is. I have heard he is a sensible man and carries no anger against Hindus in his heart.'

Father gave a small sigh. 'Bhagwan Das said the same thing. You two give me the best advice.'

'Have you asked the senior queens?'

'Rathorain will agree with whatever I say. You know what she is like, busy with her puja and never interested in politics. As for Sisodiani, ah! She is a princess of Mewar. She will never agree to such a plan. The kings of Mewar never bow before another king.'

Mother was smiling, I could make out from her voice. 'But she is your chief queen Rajaji, she should be informed.'

'I'll tell her once I return from Deosa.' Then he laughed, 'Or I'll send Bhagwan Das. She will be kinder to her son.'

Dhanibai is right, I thought. When it came to discussing the work of the kingdom, Father always came to Mother. They were still talking when I fell asleep again. The last thought I had was that even Dhanibai and Phul Kunwarji did not know anything about Father's new plans, only Mother and I did.

A royal visit

In a few days, the news of Father's plans had spread across the royal camp. The messenger he had sent to Agra came back with a letter from the Mughal king. It said that Akbar would be deeply honoured to meet Raja Bihari Mal of Amber. Khem Singh came to the zenana carrying the letter for Mother to read. I peered over Mother's shoulder to read the words written on a long roll of paper, with Akbar's royal seal at the bottom.

'Jalaluddin Akbar, Badshah of Agra and Dilli sends his greetings to His Highness,

Maharaja Bihari Mal of Amber, of the Kingdom of Dhundhar.

'We were greatly pleased to receive your message of friendship. We have been deeply grateful to His Highness for allowing us the right of passage through his kingdom to the holy pilgrimage of Ajmer Sharif, where we wish to pray at the dargah of Saint Muinuddin Chishti, may Allah bless his soul.

'Now we are deeply honoured to hear that Maharaja Bihari Mal wishes to meet us personally during our journey. Nothing would give us greater pleasure than to seek his blessings for our pilgrimage. We wait eagerly for the auspicious occasion.'

Mother read the letter very carefully and then said with approval, 'He is very polite and this is a very proper letter.'

'He has a nice handwriting,' I said, 'better than mine.'

Dhanibai laughed, 'He didn't write it, only dictated it to a clerk. I've heard he doesn't know how to read or write.'

'But he is a king!' I said, startled.

'Kings have to be good fighters and leaders, the reading and writing can be done by others,' Mother said.

Since Father's visit, Mother has been in a very good mood. Father often comes to her for advice; she sits behind the screen at the durbar while Father meets with the ministers. I know he has been planning this trip with her. Every night he sits and talks to Mother. What gifts should he take for Akbar? How big should his entourage be? Should Bhagwan Das and Man Singh go with him or not...

Sisodianiji is not happy with Father's plans but as her son the Crown Prince agrees with Father, she has not said anything, but she has not hidden her anger either. She has reminded everyone that she is a Sisodia, of the clan of Rana Sangram Singh, who fought so valiantly against Babur, Akbar's grandfather. Father stays away from her; I think he is a bit nervous of her angry words. She even said some angry things to Mother, when they met one day at the Brahma temple.

'She blames me,' Mother said to Phul

Kunwarji. 'She thinks it was my idea and I convinced Rajaji.'

'Was it your idea?' Phul Kunwarji asked curiously.

Mother shook her head. 'It was the opposite, he convinced me. Rajaji makes up his own mind. He just talks to people before he does so.'

Everyone was busy preparing for Father's trip. Gifts were gathered from many places across the kingdom. Bolts of precious silk covered in gold embroidery, rolls of cotton printed in pretty bandhani patterns, baskets of fruits, bowls and plates of silver, glass bottles of attar perfumes. Father was personally going to give Akbar a beautiful sarpech—a jewelled brooch that you fix on the turban. It was fan-shaped, like the tail of a peacock, and the gold was set with diamonds and turquoises. Mother sniffed a bit at all the expense but did not protest too much. After all, she was having such fun selecting all the gifts; she said it felt like she was collecting my wedding dowry.

Father left in a long procession, the Crown

Prince and Man Singh riding with him on elephants. Man Singh was looking very solemn wearing a turban, but catching sight of the royal women, his face split in a wide grin. He was clearly having a wonderful time. He is so lucky, he'll actually see the famous Akbar.

A fortnight later

It was afternoon and as always the women were sitting in the sun after lunch. Then Dhanibai came hurrying towards us and bent and whispered in Mother's ear and they hurried away. Radhika and I promptly followed.

A dusty horseman stood beside the gate and I recognized Khem Singh, Father's personal servant. He bowed low and handed Mother a roll of paper. 'Maharaj has sent this letter for you, Bhatiyaniji, and he said I must hand it to you personally.'

Mother took the letter and went into her tent. Radhika and I knew we wouldn't be allowed inside so we crept into our room next to it and listened. For a while there was silence and then we heard Dhani say anxiously, 'Why are you looking like that, Raniji? What has he written? Has the meeting with Akbar gone badly?'

'No,' Mother's voice was so low I could barely hear it. 'It went well. Akbar has accepted our tribute.'

'Then why are you crying?'

'Rajaji has offered Man Singh's services to Akbar and he has also offered his eldest daughter in marriage to the Mughal king.'

I froze, as Dhanibai screamed in sheer panic, 'What did you say?'

I don't know how, but I found I had entered Mother's room and saw her sitting on the carpet staring at the letter in her hands, her cheeks covered in tears. She looked up and saw me and said, 'Oh Krishna! What will I do now, Jodhi?'

I went up to her and asked, 'What has Father done, Mother?'

'He has offered your hand in marriage to Akbar, Jodhi. He has done so without even asking me.' She bent low and began to weep.

'And what has Akbar said?' Dhanibai asked.

'He has accepted the proposal. The marriage has been fixed.'

Mother, Dhanibai and Radhika were all weeping but my eyes were dry. I didn't know what to think, my body felt cold with fear but my face was all flushed and hot. I couldn't believe what I had heard. This could not be true. This must be a nightmare. I am to marry Akbar!

Mother pulled me close, hugging me tightly. Hearing her cry, the women had come in and Dhanibai told them about the letter. In the beginning, none of them could believe it. This had never been planned, they said. Father had only gone to offer his friendship and present the gifts. Rukminibai was also protesting, why was Man Singh to serve a Mughal? He is a prince. How could Jodhi marry Akbar, she is a Hindu and he a Muslim. No Amber princess has ever entered a Mughal harem...Mother sat still, looking dazed as the women chattered worriedly all around her. Some of them were hugging and kissing me but I felt nothing. Their words echoed in my head but I could not speak. All I could think of was that my marriage was fixed and instead of smiles and celebrations everyone was worried and weeping.

I don't remember much of the rest of the day. I just sat close to Mother as she, Phul Kunwarji, Rukminibai and Rathorainji discussed what they should do. Rukminibai did not want Man Singh to be away from Amber and staying in Agra. Mother did not want me to marry Akbar.

'Man Singh is only fifteen,' Rukminibai said worriedly. 'If he is in the service of Akbar, the Mughal king could send him to war and we can say nothing about it. He has no experience in fighting, he could be killed!'

'My grandson is a Rajput, he has to learn to fight, Rukmini,' Rathorainji said gently. 'He would have been sent off to war even by Rajaji. They all begin young. Rajaji was fighting in battles by Man Singh's age and I hear Akbar was leading his men at thirteen.'

'I wish I hadn't tried so hard to get him adopted,' Rukminibai muttered. 'Now he is Bhagwan Das's son and has to obey his father's wishes. No one will listen to me.'

'No one ever listens to us, don't you know that?' Rathorainji's calm face was filled with understanding. 'We are women, we can try to make the men listen to us but if they want they can forget what we say. They will always do what they want and one day, Man Singh will do that, too.'

All the while Mother had been very quiet, sitting with her head bent, staring at the carpet. Now she looked up and asked, 'Rathorainji, will my daughter have to become a Muslim?' Everyone was silent, even Rathorainji had no answer. Mother's eyes once again flooded with tears. 'If she has to convert then will she be allowed to come to Amber again? Will I be able to see my Jodh Bai again?'

Rathorainji took Mother's hand and said, 'I hear Rajaji is coming back this evening. Tonight, when he comes to the zenana, you, Rukmini and I will see him together. He has to answer our questions.' I had never seen her gentle face look so grim. 'He has to answer. I cannot let our children suffer because of his political plans. So get ready to fight for Jodh Bai.'

'What if he refuses to listen to us? He is the king.'

'He will have to listen to us,' a voice said

from the doorway. We turned in surprise, and saw the figure of Sisodianiji standing there. She had never visited our rooms before. She rarely mixed with the other women in the zenana.

Sisodianiji came and sat down beside Mother. I looked at her face. I have rarely seen her without her veil. Unlike Rathorainji and Mother, she is not beautiful, but she has a powerful face—calm, grave and a little scary. She looked around and said, 'I had feared something like this would happen. Rajaji has been too anxious to gain Akbar's friendship. I am the chief queen, the mother of the heir apparent and a Sisodia princess. I will not allow the children of Amber to be bartered in service to that Mughal because our king is afraid of war. Tonight, I sit with you.'

Mother repeated her question, 'What if he refuses to listen to us, Sisodianiji? After all, he is the king.'

'Not listen to all his queens?' A grim smile curved her thin lips. 'I don't think so. Trust me, he'll listen.'

I looked at her and thought, I have always

been a little scared of her. I thought she hates Mother but now when she said that Father will have to listen, even Mother seemed reassured. Sisodianiji turned to her maid and said, 'Go to the royal residence and leave a message with the attendant to the Maharaj that he is to visit the zenana the moment he returns.' She paused and again I saw the small, grim smile. 'And also tell his man that the queens and princesses have not eaten all day and will not do so till he visits them.'

Mother folded her hands and bowed low, touching her forehead to the floor before her. 'Thank you so much, Sisodianiji. You could have stayed away but you have come to help us. I can't express how grateful I am.'

Sisodianiji reached out and touched Mother's bent head and said softly, 'We women of the zenana only have each other, Bhatiyaniji. We have to learn to fight for our rights together.' Then she touched my cheek. 'Don't look so scared, Princess Jodh Bai. You are not married to Akbar yet.' And finally, everyone laughed and even Mother gave a small, watery smile.

Father returns

We heard his footsteps and then Father came to the door of our room, and stopped in surprise. I don't think he expected all his queens to be gathered and waiting for him in one room. He still looked dusty and tired and he must have come the moment he got the message, because he hadn't even stopped to change his clothes. I never knew the queens could summon him like this and he would oblige!

Then Father got a very unusual welcome. Usually when he enters a room, the women stand up and bow to him. Today, the three queens and Rukminibai remained seated, their faces unveiled, all looking straight up at him with cold, unsmiling faces. I sat beside Mother, her arm holding me close to her. Only Dhanibai went up and bowed before Father and invited him inside. The room was absolutely silent.

Father sat down, leaned back against a bolster and gave a faint smile. 'This is a surprise. Even you are here, Sisodianiji.'

Sisodianiji nodded. 'Someone has to take

care of the interest of the zenana when the king himself does not care.'

Father blinked, I don't think he had ever heard her speak to him like this before. 'You are all angry, I can understand that. So will you let me explain?' We all waited in silence.

Father then told us about his meeting with Akbar at Deosa. He said the Mughal camp was huge and Akbar's own tent was a very richly decorated one. It was clear to him that the Mughal king was a very powerful and rich monarch. There was a big army and the soldiers looked fit, well-trained and were good fighters. They all carried well-made weapons. Father was very impressed with the efficient arrangements in the camp and the way they were welcomed and taken to a luxuriously furnished tent and offered the best hospitality, with servants, good food and wines.

Next morning he, Bhagwan Das and Man Singh were taken to meet Akbar. Father had expected the Mughal king to be seated on a throne and had wondered if he should bow before him or not. After all, no Rajput king bows before another monarch. Instead, Akbar was waiting inside and came up to them and embraced them in welcome and personally took them to their seats.

'He treated me like an equal, not as a king who had come to offer tribute.'

'You are a king he would like as an ally,' Sisodianiji calmly interrupted Father. 'He is clever enough to understand that.' Father blinked again but did not reply directly to her comment and continued with his story.

Then all the gifts were brought in and Akbar gave even costlier gifts in return. He gave Man Singh an Arabian horse and even went riding with him. Then, he said that the Mughal army would be ready to help Amber whenever it was attacked. 'At this time I felt,' Father said, 'that I should reciprocate. So I offered Man Singh's services to Akbar. It was the right thing to do. If we are to be allies, then we should be ready to fight for each other.' He looked at Rukminibai's anxious face. 'And Man Singh agrees with me.'

'He is only fifteen and untrained in war...' Rukminibai said.

'This opportunity to train with Akbar will be good for him. Akbar has assured me he will personally make sure of Man Singh's safety. Man Singh will spend time at the Agra court learning about the work of the Mughal kingdom and he will only go on a military expedition with Akbar, never alone. And don't forget, I would have sent him to fight too, pretty soon. Now he can learn from a great general like Akbar.'

Finally Mother spoke, 'What about Jodh Bai?'

Father stayed silent for a while and then said, 'Later that day, Akbar invited me to his tent and we were alone. We talked for a long time. Then Akbar said that he wanted even closer relations with Amber and I realized he was interested in a marriage alliance. So I offered Jodhi's hand and he accepted it. If he is married to my daughter, he will be a greater ally than ever.'

'What kind of a marriage will this be?' Sisodianiji spoke. 'A Hindu marrying a Muslim? I can't imagine our child in a Mughal harem.'

'Other Hindu princesses have been married to the sultans of Dilli before. Sultan Allaudin

Khalji married the princess of Devagiri,' Father said, a bit shortly.

'But they were not marriage alliances. They were forced to marry the sultan after their kingdom had been conquered,' Sisodianiji said sharply.

Then Mother spoke bitterly, 'You lose a daughter after you lose a war, you do not offer her without a fight.'

'This will be different, it is between allies...' Father began to explain.

'And those Hindu princesses,' Sisodianiji went on relentlessly, ignoring Father, 'were forced to become Muslims and they and their children were lost to their families forever.'

'Our daughter, Jodh Bai will not have to become a Muslim.' There was a brief silence at Father's words and he continued, 'That was the first thing I asked him. I told him that the family may not agree to such a marriage if Jodhi had to convert. He promised she will not have to convert, he vowed that before me on his holy book.'

'That has never happened before,' Mother said.

'He said that he believed that everyone in his kingdom was free to follow their own religion. Jodhi will live her life her way, as a Hindu queen in the zenana.'

'How will she do that?' Rathorainji asked. 'She will have to eat their food.'

'Akbar said that Princess Jodh Bai will have her own palace with her own kitchen and temple. We are to send our own cooks and priests. She will stay away from the other zenana women and will only meet them if she wants to. She is free to do her puja, celebrate all our festivals, and she can visit us at Amber whenever she wants.'

We all looked at him in surprise. This had never happened in a Muslim king's harem before! I could live the way I liked, I could come and see Mother again?

'Think about it, Bhatiyaniji,' Father was looking at Mother. 'He is the finest groom one could find for Jodhi, if you do not refuse because of his religion. He is young, his kingdom grows every day and I spoke to him for a long time. He talks in an honest, straightforward manner and the people who know him say he is very firm about keeping his promises. I liked him.'

I realized Father was looking at me with a slight smile. 'You are my precious daughter, Jodh Bai—my eldest and most beloved. Did you think I would let you suffer in any way? I think he is the right husband for you. He is kind and well behaved, he speaks well and he is young, so you two will have much in common.' I knew he was thinking of the young princess of Bundi he had married. 'And Man Singh and his men will be there in court. You will never be alone, the people of Amber will always be around you.' He turned to Mother. 'Bhatiyaniji, will you agree to this marriage?'

Her face still and thoughtful, Mother nodded. I got up and went up to him and bent to touch his feet. Somewhere inside me, I have always trusted Father. I don't know how, but I just knew he was telling me the truth, that he would never do anything to hurt me. 'I will obey you, Rajaji,' I said formally. 'I am ready for this marriage.'

'Good.' He said pulling me close. 'You'll

make a beautiful bride, Jodh Bai, and I will cover you in jewels that the Mughals have never seen before. We will completely dazzle Akbar!' Finally reassured, the women laughed, and even Mother was smiling a little. 'Now! I hear none of you have eaten anything. Let's have dinner. I am starving.' He looked down at me. 'Tomorrow we leave for Amber. We have to prepare Jodh Bai's dowry and I can't do that without all of you helping me.'

Next morning

Everyone was still asleep when I woke and lay cuddled and warm inside my quilt. Then all the mad happenings of the day before came flooding back into my mind. I remembered I was going to marry Akbar and live in Agra.

I thought, I have to talk to Man Singh. He has seen Akbar and he can answer all those questions crowding my mind that I will never have the courage to ask Father or Mother. Man Singh has been my friend and I knew he would not lie to me. So after breakfast, I sent a maid with a message that I wanted to see him. He came immediately, as if he had been expecting my message. I was sitting on the steps by the lake waiting for him, away from Mother's eyes. He sat down beside me and grinned. 'So, Mughal Queen Jodh Bai, it looks like we are going to Agra soon.'

'You want to go there, Man Singh? Honestly?'

'Yes, very much. I want to see Agra and the Mughal court. I want to watch the way Akbar rules, then learn the art of war from him.' He threw out his arms in excitement. 'It will be such fun, Jodh Bai! Amber is such a small kingdom. Now I'll really see the world.' Watching his face, I realized he really was excited and happy at the idea of going to Agra. He was not full of fear like me. Then I remembered he would be there near me, if I was afraid.

'What's he like?'

He knew what I was talking about, 'He may be young at just twenty, but he already moves like a king. He just has to bark an order and the noblemen and soldiers run to obey him. He is not very tall, but slim and he walks quickly and rides beautifully. We went riding together and he talked quite a lot to me, asking me about my life at Amber. He laughs and jokes a lot and he even made the Crown Prince smile, and you know what a serious man he can be!' he grinned at me. 'Quite good-looking, Jodh Bai, he has a moustache but no beard, big eyes and a sharp nose. And he gave me such a fabulous black Arabian stallion! A huge, fast, wonderful horse. I have named him Bijli, as he moves like lightning.'

'He gives you a horse and you like him immediately?' I said sourly.

'Well, your gifts are going to arrive soon and I'm sure they'll be really fantastic too. Jewellery and all the stuff that girls like. I heard him tell Grandfather that he has sent a message to Agra and the gifts will be sent to Amber soon.' He gave his teasing crooked smile. 'He seemed quite excited at the idea of marrying you, actually, maybe because he has two senior queens but they are both much older than him.'

'I am scared, Man Singh,' I whispered.

'Why? I'll be there. You heard Grandfather. You'll have your own palace, all your own people around you and I will always be there whenever you need me. And Amber is not far from Agra. It is better than being married in Bikaner or Jaisalmer, far away in the desert. You are better off than the Bundi princess...' And then he gave a big, loud laugh and yelled, 'Now Jodh Bai! Remember my promise? I really have found you a young, handsome and the most powerful king!'

The Kingdom of My Father, Raja Bihari Mal *Amber – Sambhar* Winter of 1561

ONCE FATHER RETURNED FROM Deosa there was nothing to keep us at Pushkar. So we have come back to Amber as Mother is anxious to begin the preparations for my marriage. She also wants to do a special puja for me.

Once again back within the familiar walls of the zenana, it all felt a bit odd. I am suddenly very important. Till now, I was just one of the princesses and allowed to grow up in the zenana deori among all the other girls. Now, I am addressed as Rajkumari Jodh Bai, an important princess who is going to marry the Mughal King, Akbar. Everyone is looking at me differently and the other girls had many questions to ask. Even Radhika was bombarding me with them. What is Badshah Akbar like? What is the Mughal harem like and is it different from our zenana deori? When I move to the harem, will I have to pray five times every day? Why don't they understand that I don't know much. It's all new for me too.

The days go by in a whirl of preparations for the wedding. The plan is that after Akbar has done his pilgrimage at Ajmer, the marriage will be held when he is on his way back to Agra. Father says we will wait for him at a place called Sambhar, on the road from Ajmer to Agra. There the marriage will be held and then Man Singh and I will travel in Akbar's entourage to Agra. So we have only a few weeks to prepare for the wedding and then travel to Sambhar. It is driving Mother, Dhanibai and Phul Kunwarji quite frantic with worry about getting my dowry ready on time.

I spend all day getting measured by the

tailors, then sitting with the seamstresses who embroider the clothes, selecting the designs; and with the jewellers and the perfume makers. The weavers carry in bolts of cloth, the printers send us patterns, people selling silver vessels, furniture, kitchen utensils are all waiting for us at the zenana deori gate. I never knew planning a wedding could be such a complicated thing. I am quite exhausted at the end of the day!

In one corner of the deori the seamstresses have settled down, stitching and embroidering my clothes. All the women in the deori will get new lehengas, cholis and chunaris for the wedding. The women sit bent over the cloth, their needles flying, working late into the night. Whenever I go and sit with them, they tease me and keep calling me Begum Sahiba.

Mother and I spend hours brooding over lengths of silk and cotton, wondering about designs to be embroidered. I chose many pieces of soft mulmul tie-dyed with the pretty dots of the bandhani pattern to be stitched into cholis and made into chunaris. It really helps to have Phul Kunwarji around because using a charcoal, she draws the designs on paper to show the women what I want. Mother wanted most of my clothes to be in shades of red and yellow but I refused and chose many blues and greens. Phul Kunwarji agrees with me that I look nicer in softer colours.

The days go by quickly as I am surrounded by people but at night when I lie tired in bed, all my fears come crowding back into my mind. I hardly think of Akbar during the day but at night I try to remember what Man Singh told me about him. It helps to know that Father and Man Singh like him, but will he like me? I know I am not beautiful like Mother, though Phul Kunwarji says I am pretty. But there is a big difference between 'pretty' and 'beautiful'. I dance quite well but I can't really sing. I sometimes get up and study my face in the mirror wishing my eyes were larger, my nose a bit different. Kings marry many times and the Mughal harem will be full of beautiful Persian and Turkish women with fair skins and light eyes. I was so afraid of getting lost and forgotten among them, like Phul Kunwarji has been in the zenana deori.

A look into my future

Pandit Omkar Narain is our royal priest, astrologer and a very important man. Father does not do anything without consulting him. Now he was called into the zenana deori to look at Akbar's and my horoscopes. Mother is still worried about my future. Also, she and Father wanted him to pick an auspicious date for the wedding. Father had got Akbar's exact date of birth and asked Panditji to draw our horoscope charts.

Father, Mother and I sat before him. Mother and I had veiled ourselves. He is an old, white-haired man, dressed in spotless white dhoti-kurta, with the stripes of sandalwood marks drawn across his forehead, with a big red dot of a tika in the middle. He has a long, drooping white moustache and his sharp, large eyes seem to notice everything. I like him because he listens to what everyone says and speaks very kindly. Now, he unrolled two long strips of paper on which he had drawn the charts of two horoscopes–Akbar's and mine. On top of each strip was the diagram of the horoscope, showing the position of the stars at our birth, and below were rows of words.

'Do they match, Panditji?' Father asked anxiously.

He nodded with a satisfied smile. 'They match very well.' And then he talked of the stars, of Shani and Rahu, Brihaspati and Mangal and how Akbar and I were going to be good for each other. That the marriage was good for Amber and Agra and I would bring fame and riches to both.

'Panditji...' Mother spoke from behind her veil, 'Will our daughter Jodh Bai be happy?'

'Yes, she will be,' he said firmly, 'let me assure you of this, Bhatiyaniji. I know you are worried about this marriage. After all, Amber has never agreed to such an unusual marriage alliance before. Even I was worried in the beginning, till I took a look at the horoscopes.' He pointed to one of the rolls of paper. 'I like his horoscope. He is a good man and he will be good to your daughter.'

'It is a Muslim harem and...' Mother began.

'Yes. That is why a separate palace is good.

Our princess will live and eat in the Hindu way. And Bhatiyaniji, I am sending my eldest son to Agra as the personal priest for the princess. He will make sure everything is done correctly. Then no one will have anything to criticize about her staying in Akbar's zenana.'

'You see any future conflict between Agra and Amber?' Father asked.

'None. This is the beginning of a great friendship, Rajaji, and it will go on for many generations. It is also the best for Prince Man Singh.' Then he smiled at me. 'And Princess, let me tell you, it will be a pleasure to be the priest at your wedding.'

Mother suddenly sat up at Panditji's last words and exclaimed, 'Oh Krishna! The wedding ceremony! How do we hold a ceremony of a Hindu and a Muslim? I cannot allow Jodh Bai to marry Akbar in a Muslim ceremony and he will not agree to a Hindu one.'

'I asked Akbar about that too,' Father said. 'He said for him all religious ceremonies are the same. He is quite willing to sit before the fire...'

'But how can he? He is a Muslim!' Mother

protested angrily. 'And no priest will agree to perform the rituals.' She gave an irritated glare at Father. 'Rajaji, how can we agree to marriage proposals without thinking about them properly? Even if Akbar sits before the fire, will he recite the mantras? Will the priest let him do so?'

We looked enquiringly at Panditji who sat there looking both thoughtful and worried. 'Ah! This is a truly great problem...'

'See!' Mother exclaimed. 'We can't have this marriage. I will not allow my Jodh Bai to undergo a Muslim nikaah ceremony. I just won't!'

Father was staring sternly at Panditji. 'You have to find a solution, now! It is too late to back away, he has already sent Jodh Bai's wedding trousseau. I can't take the risk of angering Akbar and cancelling the wedding.'

'Can we consider Akbar to be a Rajput?' Panditji asked, as the three of us stared at him feeling puzzled. 'He is a king after all and all kings are considered to be Rajputs...' He went on thoughtfully. 'This can be a marriage of two Rajputs before a fire. He does not have to recite any mantras, we will recite them for him. We will place his sword beside the bride, so he won't sit there. He will only have to sit before the fire when you give her away.'

'There!' Father said with a relieved laugh, 'Now there is no problem.' Mother did not quite look happy, but did not argue any more.

Panditji got up to leave and then stopped to look at me. 'Rajkumari, I see great things for you in the future. If this old priest knows anything about the stars, then you will be a queen the people will never forget.'

I felt much calmer after that and I realized, so did Mother. We all believe Panditji always speaks the truth because there have been many times when he has even opposed Father's decisions. If he said I'll be happy, then maybe I will be. Even though I am not smart or beautiful.

My trousseau is prepared

I had been summoned to the baithak to select the jewellery. Father, Mother, Phul Kunwarji and Dhanibai were also in the sitting room. No one wanted to miss the treat. As we sat, with us women veiling our faces, the biggest jewellers, not just from our kingdom but also from Jodhpur, Bikaner, Ajmer and even far-off Dilli and Kashi came in to show us their best pieces.

I sat dazzled as they opened box after box of necklaces and bangles, earrings, anklets, bracelets, rings, nose rings, hair clips, waistbands and even jewelled toe rings! The ones we liked were kept back and Father wrote a chit for the munshi to make payments. Some jewellery was also bought for Badshah Akbar—a six-strand pearl necklace, bracelets for the wrist and bands for the upper arm, small earrings and a set of ornaments for the turban, the sarpech.

'This will take me years to wear!' I laughed at Father.

'They are only for the first year.' He grinned back. 'On every festival, I'll send you more. And when you give Akbar a son, just wait and see the gifts that we send to Agra!' I felt my face grow hot in confusion as Mother laughed.

Then one day Mother, Sisodianiji and Rathorainji sat down to decide who will travel with me to Agra and stay with me there. Like

Dhanibai had come from Jaisalmer with Mother, I am going to have a personal entourage from the zenana. The senior maid is going to be Chandabai, an old friend of Dhanibai. I like her, she is much kinder than her friend.

'Jodh Bai will have a separate palace,' Sisodianiji said, 'and will need a lady-in-waiting to manage everything.'

Mother looked thoughtful, 'The lady-in-waiting will have to be of noble blood.'

Phul Kunwarji spoke up, 'Can I go as Jodh Bai's lady-in-waiting, Bhatiyaniji?'

'How can you?' Mother said. 'You are the wife of a prince, Phul Kunwarji.'

'A prince who has forgotten me. I am of noble blood but I am not a queen, never will be. And what is my fate? To end my life in the old deori among the forgotten women? Instead of spending these empty days I would rather help Jodh Bai in her new role. She is young and will need help learning to live in a strange zenana.'

'Oh please, please Mother,' I pleaded, 'let Phul Kunwarji come with me.'

'I don't know if Rajaji...' Mother began doubtfully.

'Leave this to me,' Rathorainji said. 'It is an excellent idea and don't worry, I'll get Rajaji to agree to it. I'm sure he will not refuse me.'

So that's how I discovered that I really would have friends and family around me in Agra: Phul Kunwarji, Chandabai and Man Singh, of course. Then I discovered that Father was also sending his personal servant Khem Singh as the head of the guards! I was beginning to feel much better.

Leaving for Sambhar

The messengers rode between Amber and Ajmer every day carrying messages between Father and Akbar. So we knew he was spending time at the saint's shrine in prayer. Then he sent a message that he would meet us at Sambhar in a fortnight and I felt my heart thud. A fortnight! Oh Krishna! It was going to be so soon?

We were all ready to travel. The next day the rows of bullock and camel carts, palanquins, horses and elephants left in a procession for

Sambhar. The royal camp had to be all ready to receive Akbar when he arrived.

A week later, the Mughals arrived. Man Singh came excitedly into our tent and said, 'Badshah Akbar is here, Bhatiyaniji!' and I went hot and cold and had to stay very still to stop my head from spinning.

Everything was ready for the wedding, as it was to take place two days later. The trays of gifts from Akbar were carried into our camp—bolts of silk, velvet boxes of jewellery, rolls of carpets. We were told that this is just the beginning, that the king's mother and aunt have prepared a much larger array that is waiting for me in Agra. There was a special request from Akbar that I should select one item from the jewellery he had sent for me and wear it at the wedding.

All the women laughed when they heard of Badshah Akbar's message. 'Ah! Princess. Your betrothed is very romantic,' teased Dhanibai.

'Select a nose ring,' someone said, 'then you will have to raise your veil to show him that you are wearing it.' I knew I was blushing as I finally selected a pair of pearl and ruby bangles.

He will see my arms during the ceremony, I thought.

The night before the wedding, I lay there, sleepless in bed, thinking of what was about to take place. Even a few months ago, I had not imagined that I would one day marry a Mughal king. I was at times quite happy about it, at others, full of fear. I remember what the message from Akbar said, that his mother and aunt were preparing gifts for me. They would be the senior queens in the harem and I wondered whether they were happy to get a Hindu daughter-in-law. Man Singh had found out their names too–Akbar's mother was Hamida Banu Begum, senior wife of Akbar's father, the late Mughal king, Humayun and his aunt was Humayun's sister, Gulbadan Begum.

What Man Singh had also told me was that Akbar already had two senior queens and that I was going to be like my mother, a junior queen. 'Two wives!' I asked worriedly. 'Oh no!'

'Yes. Salima Sultan and Ruqayya Begum. I think Salima Sultan is also his cousin.'

'He must have married them when they were

very young. After all he is barely twenty himself,' I said, imagining two young queens who would not be happy at all at his getting a Hindu wife. I remembered how Sisodianiji had been unkind to Mother.

'I think both of them are older than him. These queens were married to him some years ago when he was still a teenager.'

'Does he have children?'

Man Singh shook his head, 'I don't think so.'

So I had a mother-in-law, an aunt-in-law and two senior queens to face, I thought nervously, lying there staring up at the roof of the tent. It is lucky I will have my own palace, where I can hide from them if they are being unkind to me. Oh! I wish Mother and Dhanibai could come with me, even for a few months. Mother told me that after her marriage, it was three years before she could go home to visit her parents. Jaisalmer is very far from Amber and there was a war going on. I wondered when I would be allowed to come to Amber and see Mother and Radhika again.

I already miss my life in Amber—the room

I share with Radhika, the courtyard where we played, the corner of the veranda where I sit and dream over my bahi khata. Then I thought, I have to tell Dhanibai to remember to feed my pigeons, Radhi will never remember...

My wedding day

My wedding clothes are so heavy. The deep red skirt of the lehenga, made of thick silk is stiff with gold embroidery and set with tiny pearls and it weighs a ton. The choli blouse on top is also embroidered. The veil of the chunari is made of a gossamer thin gold cloth and embroidered in gold thread. I will lower it over my face when I go into the wedding tent.

Yesterday, Phul Kunwarji had drawn the intricate red henna designs on my palms and feet. Now I slipped on the gold bracelets set with diamonds and Dhanibai tied the armbands on my upper arms. Radhika slipped on three rings and then the heavy silver anklets. Mother helped me put on the heavy ruby and seed pearl earrings that dangled to my shoulders and then a short necklace, a longer one and also a row of chains that fell across my chest. A heavy silver belt was tied to my waist. Finally I put on the pearl and ruby bangles that Akbar had sent me. Phul Kunwarji had reddened my palms with lac, lined my eyes with kohl and sprayed me with attar perfume. She had plaited my hair with gold thread and then placed the gold chain of the tika along the parting of my hair, with the pendant dangling over my forehead.

With all the heavy clothes and jewellery I couldn't get up! They had to help me stand and I took small steps while walking, everything swishing and clinking as I moved. Radhika ran up with a large mirror and I looked at my reflection and thought, 'Oh! I look so grown-up!'

'You look so beautiful, Jodhi!' Radhika breathed as Dhanibai made the sign of warding off evil over my head and sniffed away her tears. I looked up from the mirror and saw Mother's face, she was smiling a little but her eyes were shiny with tears. She said nothing, just kissing me gently, her soft hands stroking my cheeks. I understood a little what she felt. Radhika and I were all she had in that lonely zenana deori and now I am going away. Soon it will be Radhika's turn.

I walked to the marriage tent, surrounded by women, everyone veiled and singing wedding songs. In the tent, Dhanibai led me to the seat before the holy fire. During the first rituals, only my groom Akbar's sword was kept on the seat beside me and the priests recited the mantras for him. I think he was somewhere in the tent watching everything because I heard someone being addressed as 'Your Royal Highness' by Bhagwan Das and an unfamiliar voice replied. I could see nothing through the thick veil except my own feet and the floor before me.

Akbar came to sit in front of me, across the fire, for the ritual when Father gave me away. We sat facing each other with Pandit Omkar Narain and Father on each side. I heard the rustle of his clothes as he sat down and then a whiff of attar and Panditji was saying something to him about whether he could put a tika on his forehead.

'Please go ahead,' said Akbar. 'I would like to wear the tika.' Then Father placed my hand in his and I realized Akbar was cold too, his hand was icy and, feeling my hand shake, he held it tightly for a moment. We walked around the fire and all I could see were his feet. Fair, narrow feet and the edge of his churidar trousers. I wondered if he noticed that I was wearing the bangles he had sent for me.

It was late in the night when the ceremony finished and I was so tired I could barely walk. The women helped me up and I walked back in a daze. As they chattered while taking off the jewellery, I only remembered one thing that Dhanibai whispered to me as I slid thankfully under the quilt, 'I like his face, Rani Jodh Bai, and he speaks with great courtesy.' And then I was asleep.

Kingdom of Jalaluddin Akbar
The Mughal Fortress, Agra
1562

WE HAVE BEEN TRAVELLING FOR days from Sambhar to Agra. Phul Kunwarji, Chandabai and I travelled in a covered bullock cart. We were always surrounded by Rajput horsemen and often, Man Singh rode in front of us. I sat and watched the changing landscape through the parted curtains. After the scrub and desert of my land, it is so green here, with fields of yellow mustard and golden wheat. As we passed the villages the people ran out to see the royal procession. I wondered what they thought about their Badshah's new Rajput wife.

All day we travelled and at night camp was set. We moved quite slowly, sometimes staying at one place for a few days as Akbar met local noblemen or went hunting. Every day his personal valet comes to ask if we are comfortable and if we need anything. Yesterday, he brought a basket of apples and oranges, and this morning a pretty engraved silver box 'for the Ranibai to keep her paan,' said the valet, making Chandabai smile. 'Does your king like paan? Then the Ranibai can send some to him,' Chandabai asked.

The valet bowed and nodded, so Phul Kunwarji and I sent a tray of sweet, green paan, fragrant with spices. Later, after lunch, the valet came back with the message that Akbar had liked the paan very much, and would Rani Jodh Bai send these every day? So I make paan for him every morning. One day, I'll cook the best royal Amber dishes for him.

The days pass but at night I lie awake thinking of Mother, Radhika, Father and Dhanibai, of my home in Amber, my pigeons, even of Sukhwanti Bai, who was probably still teaching Radhika and the other girls. I miss them so much but if I weep, no one sees my tears. After all, a Rajput princess never cries before people.

Yesterday morning, Man Singh was riding beside our cart and chatting with me when another horseman rode up and moved casually beside him. Then I saw Man Singh bow. Phul Kunwarji peered over my shoulder and said, 'That's King Akbar! Jodh Bai, look!'

I parted the curtain and looked out for the first sight of my husband. He is not handsome and has quite plain features, but he rides well. The thin eyebrows curve above large eyes, the nose is a bit beaky and a dark brown moustache droops over full lips. There is a small mole above his lips. He knew I was watching him and said to Man Singh, 'I came to see if the Princess is comfortable.'

Man Singh just grinned and nodded. I opened the curtain wider so he could see my unveiled face and as he stared at me for a moment, I raised an arm and showed him that I was wearing the bangles he had sent me. He laughed, bowed and then rode away. At least now I will recognize him when I see him next, I thought in relief.

From what I could see through the small opening in the curtains, the fort at Agra is much larger than the one in Amber. It is not on a hill, instead it stands beside the Yamuna river. Tall, stone gateways lead into the main palaces. I was taken to a small palace in a corner of the women's quarters. They call it the haramsara or the mahal and it is very much like our zenana deori. Chandabai and Phul Kunwarji busied themselves with the unpacking, placing the furniture and supervising the kitchen, and I wandered from room to room thinking this is my home now for the rest of my life.

The rooms have carved and painted walls, and carpets cover the floors. The furnishing is similar to Amber but everything appears richer. Deeper carpets, expensive silk bolsters, silver bowls and lamps. I walked up the stairs to the first floor terrace and looked around. All the harem palaces lay behind a high wall and I saw the guards at the doors. At my palace, Khem

Singh lounged against a pillar chewing paan. My palace! I thought, that feels so strange.

Then I heard the soft, deep cooing at my feet and looked down. Pigeons! There were pigeons! I ran down to the kitchen to get a bowl of grain. Oh! The pigeons made me feel so good as they strutted up to peck the grain from my hand. Now I can keep pigeons even here.

Meeting the harem women

Next morning, Phul Kunwarji and Chandabai fussed, getting me ready. Today the senior queens of the harem were coming to see me. The wedding dress and jewellery were all brought out again and I sat there as they worked on my hair and face using henna, kohl and lac. I was told that I was to sit with my face uncovered because the women wanted to see how I looked.

I sat on the carpet in the middle of the sitting room as the harem women gathered around me. Then two older women entered and Phul Kunwarji whispered, 'The queen mother and the aunt! Touch their feet.' As they came closer, I reached forward and touched their feet. They looked a bit surprised; probably Muslims do not do that.

The older woman with greying hair and a stern face sat down before me saying briskly, 'So you are Jodh Bai!' A hand held my chin and raised my face. 'Pretty enough for my son.' So this was the Queen Mother, Hamida Banu Begum. 'But if you are so shy before him, he'll lose interest,' she added, making the women laugh. She gave me a set of jewellery and as I whispered my thanks she said, 'Don't whisper, child, I can't hear a word you are saying!'

Gulbadan Begum, Akbar's aunt, had a kinder face and said with a laugh, 'Hush Hamida! You are scaring the child. Don't you remember your own wedding day anymore?'

'My wedding day was nothing like this. His Majesty never gave me a palace of my own and a room full of clothes and jewellery.'

Just then, all the women turned towards the door and Phul Kunwarji whispered, 'The queens!' I looked up nervously. The first to come forward was Salima Sultan who was Akbar's cousin. She has sharp, fair features and odd grey eyes. Unlike Hamida Banu and Gulbadan, she did not even bother to smile. A rough hand held my chin and raised my face. 'This is a child! Since when has Badshah Akbar liked children?' Then she looked at me. 'I hope he does not forget you, Princess.'

The other queen, Ruqayya Begum laughed, 'And a Hindu too. Imagine marrying a girl from a village in the desert.'

That made me look up and I raised my voice and said politely, 'Begum Sahiba, we are the Rajput rulers from Amber. I am of royal blood.'

The room was still and silent for a moment and then Gulbadan laughed, 'Ah! So you can talk, Jodh Bai! You do have some spirit.'

I looked down at the boxes of jewellery the queens had given me and said the way Mother had taught me, 'I thank you for your gifts. I will always treasure them.'

Phul Kunwarji and Chandabai came in carrying gifts for all the four royal women and I realized they were impressed by the expensive lengths of silk and the pearl necklaces. They had not expected a small kingdom like Amber to give such expensive gifts. As the women sat chatting, sipping sherbet and eating the sweets, I looked at their faces. They looked a little different from the women in the zenana deori—fairer, some with brownish hair and pale eyes but they spoke of the same things, gossiped and teased, argued and laughed in the same way.

Only Gulbadan took the trouble to talk to me. 'Do not take their unkind words to heart, child,' she said gently. 'The mahal is a cruel place. You have to be proud and brave but I think you'll succeed. I don't think you'll let them trouble you.'

'You are kind, Begum Sahiba. I thank you for that.'

'Well, I like your pretty manners and I think Akbar will like them too. And if you ever need any help come to me.'

That afternoon

It was afternoon and everyone was taking a nap after lunch but I could not sleep. I went up to the first floor terrace with a bowl of grain and sat feeding the pigeons. Like at Amber, once I get familiar with the birds that come regularly, I'll start talking to them, telling them of the happenings of the day, all my hopes and dreams, my innermost thoughts. At Amber I had my favourite, a white pigeon with flecks of black on the wings, who was the bravest and always came right up to me to peck grain from my hand. She would patter happily around my feet like a little busybody and look up at me with her red eyes as if she understood everything I said. I called her Sitara, my star, and I missed her.

'You like pigeons, Princess?' a voice said behind me, and I turned to see Akbar standing behind me.

I nodded. 'I had pigeons in Amber.'

'White or grey?'

'Mostly lotan and the small goli pigeons.'

'Oh!' he laughed. 'So you really know about pigeons.' He held out his hand. 'Then come with me and see my pigeons. There is the latest pair I have got from Kabul, they are pale grey and fly like angels.' And holding my hand he pulled me along down the stairs and out of my palace. As we walked out he looked at me and said, 'And Jodh Bai, you don't have to veil your face! This is the zenana and here you walk freely.' His smile deepened. 'And I want to look at your face.' As we walked along the gardens towards his palace he said, 'Are you always called Rajkumari Jodh Bai?'

I shook my head. 'The family calls me Jodhi.' I turned to look at him, 'What do I call you? You are always Badshah Akbar?'

'Always. Unless you want to call me Badshah salamat, Your Highness!'

I laughed, 'My Father is called Rajaji, so you are Badshahji.'

'Hmm, not a bad name. Actually I prefer it to Akbar.'

By then we had walked up to the terrace of his palace and I saw that one wall was covered with pigeon houses and cages. 'You even have cages! I always wanted them but they said girls don't keep pigeons.'

'I'll get some made for you. Then you can see them nest and watch the baby pigeons grow up and train them properly.'

We crouched before the cages and hearing

us, the birds inside became curious and poked their heads out to look at us, cooing and muttering away, making me laugh. Pigeons can look so pretty and so stupid at the same time. He brought out the special pair from Kabul. They were a lovely pale grey and I stroked the soft silky feathers and said, 'They are beautiful. What are they called?'

'They are gerobaaz pigeons and I have named them Badal and Ghata.'

'Clouds! Of course!' I smiled at him. 'I like the names, grey like the monsoon clouds.'

He let a white pigeon hop on to his arm. 'This one's my favourite. I call her Chandani, as she is white as the moonlight.'

'My favourite was a white one with flecks of black. I called her Sitara because the flecks were like tiny stars. She also came and sat on my arm and would even sit in my lap.'

Akbar let the pigeons out of the cages and flew them for me. They wheeled and fluttered above our heads as we stood there calling to them. He saw me reach out and get a pigeon to come and sit on my hand and said, 'You are good with them. Maybe we should appoint you my royal kabutarbaaz.'

'What's a kabutarbaaz?'

'My keeper of pigeons. You know how to make them obey you, so you will be good at training them. And I have to get another pair,' he smiled down at me, 'white with flecks of black.'

'What will you call them?'

'Jodh Bai and Akbar?' he asked, making me smile, 'What do you think, my kabutarbaaz?'

Suddenly I felt all my fears fall away. I know it is going to be all right, I just know it. For the first time I have started feeling hopeful and happy, as the pigeons wheel around Akbar and me in a joyous cloud of fluttering wings.

The Real Jodh Bai in History

IN JANUARY 1562, THE PRINCESS of Amber became the first Hindu princess to marry the Mughal King, Akbar. All the histories written at that time mention the marriage but interestingly none of them tell us her name! She is just referred to as the 'Princess of Amber' or the 'Daughter of Raja Bihari Mal of Amber'.

So how do we know her name was really Jodh Bai? Actually, we don't. Many historians studying the family tree of the Kachhwahas of Amber think she was called Harkha Bai. There is no Jodh Bai to be found in the list of princesses. The royal histories first call her the Princess of Amber and then refer to her as Mariam-us-Zamani, the title that Akbar bestowed on her when she gave birth to his first son. In those days royalty had many titles, so Jodh, Jodha, Harkha Bai or Mariam-us-Zamani, she is a woman people have not forgotten.

Akbar was twenty-six when Jodh Bai gave him his first living son and heir, Prince Salim. This immediately made her the most important queen in the Mughal harem. After Akbar's death, Salim became king, taking the title of Jahangir, and Jodh Bai as Queen Mother became the head of the harem. Many of the Mughal queens and princesses had their portraits painted, but sadly there are no miniature paintings of Jodh Bai.

After Jodh Bai, many other Hindu Rajput princesses were married to the Mughals. Salim married Man Singh's sister Mani Bai, who became the mother of Prince Khusro. Two Jodhpur princesses were also married into the Mughal family. All of them were allowed to practice their religion freely within the harem.

However, the Sisodia clan of Mewar never agreed to a marriage alliance with the Mughals.

Jodh Bai and Akbar must have been quite close as he used to join in all the Hindu festivals celebrated in her palace. He loved to play Holi, the festival of colours, and celebrated Deepavali with lights and fireworks. He also grew his hair, tied it in a Rajasthani style turban and enjoyed putting a tika on his forehead. It is said that Jodh Bai taught him to chew paan!

Jodh Bai's fears that she would become a forgotten wife did not come true. She and Akbar must have become good companions because she was a regular adviser to him and he trusted her judgement. She became a powerful queen and even today, some of the royal orders, called firmans, signed by her have survived. She was also a good businesswoman and owned fields of indigo. She traded in these with Europe. She managed to do all this while living in purdah in the harem. She sat behind a screen and met her business managers and listened to people coming with requests.

When Akbar built his new capital city of Fatehpur Sikri near Agra, he built a separate palace for his Hindu queen and it is still called Jodh Bai's palace. This palace is the biggest and most beautiful in the harem area. The tourist guides also point to another smaller building and say it was her kitchen where she cooked for Akbar. Of course that could be just a fancy tale! The rooms are around an open courtyard and in the middle of the open space is a stone stand where they say Jodh Bai grew her tulsi plant for worship.

Man Singh too became a famous and trusted general of Akbar. He fought many wars and was sent to Bengal as the governor. As a Mughal nobleman he became very rich and used his wealth to build many new palaces at Amber. He was one of the most successful kings of the Amber dynasty. Later, one of his descendants, Jai Singh II, built the city of Jaipur on the plains right below Amber and shifted his capital there. Man Singh's beautiful palaces at Amber still survive on top of the hill near Jaipur.

Jodh Bai lived a long and rich life. Both

she and Man Singh survived Akbar who died in 1605. She died during the reign of her son Jahangir, and her memorial was built by him near Akbar's mausoleum at Sikandra in Agra.

ALSO IN THIS SERIES

THE TEENAGE DIARY OF JAHANARA

SUBHADRA SEN GUPTA

I, Jahanara, a Mughal princess, want to keep a record of everything that happens in my life...

It is 1626, and Jahanara is in Mandu, central India. Her father, Prince Khurram–who will later become Emperor Shah Jahan–has fallen out of favour with Emperor Jahangir, and now lives in the Deccan with his wife Arjamand Bano and their five children. As events unfold around her, Jahanara records them in her diary–her father's reaction to his exile; Empress Nur Jahan's demand that Jahanara's brothers be sent to her court as hostages; the conspiracies in faraway Agra and Lahore as Jahangir slides into ill-health; her own growth as a sensitive writer and poet. Then one day, her father rides away to capture the Mughal throne, paving the way for Jahanara to return to her beloved Agra.

This fictional diary recreates the drama of ambition, intrigue and loyalty that marked the Mughal empire at the height of its glory. As young Jahanara witnesses her father's rise to the throne, she also contemplates the incredible cruelty that men inflict on each other, and the love and tenderness that will finally redeem all. Gripping and lyrical, *The Teenage Diary of Jahanara* brings to life a time we only read about in history books.

ALSO IN THIS SERIES

THE TEENAGE DIARY OF NUR JAHAN

DEEPA AGARWAL

Long before she became Nur Jahan—Emperor Jahangir's last wife and the most influential Mughal queen—she was Mehr-un-nissa. Born to Persian refugees who attained eminence at the Mughal court, Mehr-un-nissa grew up on the fringes of Emperor Akbar's court in Agra, Kabul and Lahore.

In this fictional diary, Deepa Agarwal gives us a glimpse into the queen's teenage years: how she grows into a strong and passionate young woman; her love for poetry and writing; and her interest in the larger world around her. Her diary also describes the Mughal world through the eyes of a young girl: the vibrant Meena Bazaars; the elaborate festival celebrations; and the intricacies of life in the zenana. But above all, her diary records her ambition to meet the love of her life and also to carve a place for herself in history.

A fascinating blend of history and fiction, *The Teenage Diary of Nur Jahan* brings alive a bygone age in a unique and captivating manner for young readers.